Boost Spelling Skills 3

Strategies, Tips and Practice Activities to Help Upper KS2 Pupils Develop and Improve Word Pattern Recognition

Judy Arden

Judy Arden (Thornby) is an experienced former primary teacher and specialist in learning support. She has taught pupils with a range of abilities for over 25 years, gaining a Diploma in Specific Learning Difficulties in 1999. Being enthusiastic about promoting literacy skills, she has written the *'Boost Spelling Skills'* series for KS1 and KS2, and older pupils who struggle with spelling. She has also written the *'Boost Creative Writing Skills'* series.

Published by Brilliant Publications Limited
Unit 10
Sparrow Hall Farm
Edlesborough
Dunstable
Bedfordshire
LU6 2ES, UK

www.brilliantpublications.co.uk

Brilliant Publications is a registered trademark.

Written by Judy Arden
Illustrations: Brilliant Publications Limited
Cover: Molly Sage

Printed ISBN: 978-0-85747-986-0
PDF ISBN: 978-0-85747-988-4
First printed and published in the UK in 2023
10 9 8 7 6 5 4 3 2 1

Contents

Introduction

hip/po/pot/am/us Spelling Strategies

Keywords

changeable Suffixes

Contents

Dictation Exercises

peaceful

Functions of Suffixes

misfortune

Prefixes

Dictation Exercises

extraction

Root Words

Contents

signalling

Spelling Rules

Dictation Exercises

sail/sale

Homophones

Dictation Exercises

gnome

Silent Letters

Dictation Exercises

Introduction

About the Book

Boost Spelling Skills 3 is designed for use at upper KS2 level and can also be used by older pupils who find spelling challenging. The book follows DFES National Literacy guidelines for spelling for the 9–11 years age group and is divided into nine sections:

1. Strategies
2. Keywords
3. Suffixes
4. Functions of suffixes
5. Spelling rules for adding suffixes
6. Prefixes
7. Root words
8. Homophones
9. Silent Letters

Boost Spelling Skills 3 extends the various strategies taught in the infant school to help pupils improve their spelling. These strategies include using 'memory joggers', looking for smaller words within longer ones (to identify and help the pupil spell the tricky part of a word) and splitting a longer difficult word into bite size pieces. A '*Look, Say, Cover, Write, Check*' (LSCWC) pro forma is included as this is a tried and trusted strategy to promote good spelling skills, by using visual auditory and kinaesthetic cues in a multisensory approach. The recognition of unstressed vowels in words (such as memorable or interested) is another useful spelling aid which is taken into consideration.

A focus of the book is to investigate prefixes, roots or base words and suffixes which are the building blocks of words. It explores how suffixes and prefixes can modify the meaning and spelling of the word. Adding a suffix can change a word into an adjective, noun or adverb as well as changing the tense of a word. Many words have their origins in Latin or Greek. It is helpful to identify the meaning of some word roots as it extends vocabulary and assists spelling. For example the root '*annus*' comes from the Latin word meaning year and can be noticed in words such as 'annual', 'anniversary' and 'annuity'. Research shows pupils who have a good understanding of word structures tend to have better spelling and reading comprehension skills.

There is emphasis on the main spelling rules that apply when adding suffixes which include the **double consonant** rule, **'e'** rule and **'y'** rules. Developing knowledge of these rules will give an understanding of how the spelling of the base word can change when adding a suffix, although there are always some exceptions to these rules.

Introduction

The book contains lists of spellings, reading activities and worksheets which provide reinforcement to each specific letter pattern, suffix/prefix ending or spelling rule covered. In the reading passages the pupil is asked to highlight the target letter pattern whilst reading. Targeted dictation exercises at different stages and spelling games provide further opportunity for consolidation.

Sections on homophones and silent letters build on the work covered at KS1 level. It is important to have awareness of silent letters, as they are prominent in the English language and are present in about 60% of our vocabulary, affecting more than half the letters of the alphabet.

Spelling Strategies

Different Strategies

There are various helpful ways in which you can boost spelling:

Teacher's Tips

Invent a mnemonic or memory jogger to help with the spelling of whole or parts of trickier words. Children love to make up silly phrases!

For example: **build:**

big **u**gly **i**guanas **l**ove **d**ogs

Become a Word Detective: Look for smaller words inside longer words.

For example:

vegetable = **get, table, able**

business = **bus, sin, in**

Notice compound words.

For example:

heavyweight: heavy / weight

somewhere: some / where

knowledge: know / ledge

Spelling Strategies

hip/po/pot/am/us

Teacher's Tips

Split the words into syllables – bite size pieces are easier to recall.

For example: **hippopotamus**

hip/po/pot/am/us

Identify unstressed vowels /uh/ sound.

For example:

memorable **interested**

marvellous

Take an irregularly spelt word and say it wrongly – pronounce it exactly how it looks.

For example:

Wed-nes-day **bus-in-ess**

Use a

'Look, Say, Cover, Write, Check'

approach when learning new spellings.

Spelling Strategies

Teacher's Tips

Spot the prefix and the suffix to identify the root/base word.

For example: **disappointment**

dis / appoint / ment

Link words with the same root.

For example:

act :

actor : action : extract : contact : reaction : abstract : factory : attraction

Spelling Strategies

Look, Say, Cover, Write, Check

LOOK 	at the word carefully. Can you see a smaller word in it? Is there a tricky bit? Notice if there is a prefix or suffix.
SAY 	the word out loud. How many syllables does it have?
COVER 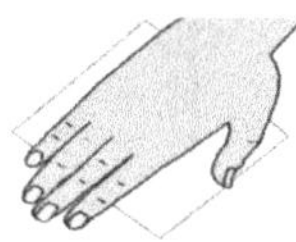	the word up when you think you have remembered it.
WRITE 	the word down without looking.
CHECK  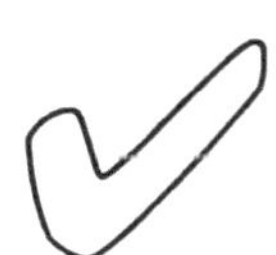	Have you written the word correctly? Repeat again five times.

Guidelines

Look at the word and make a picture of it in your head. Say the word out loud then cover it up before writing it down. Let the movement of the pen help the memory of the shape of the word. Finally check if it has been spelt correctly. Correct if needed and write again. This is an effective way of imprinting the word to memory as it uses a multisensory approach. Multisensory learning involves visual, auditory and kinaesthetic tactile prompts and is a helpful strategy for all pupils. A 'Look, Say, Cover, Write, Check' pro forma is on the next pages (12-13).

hip/po/pot/am/us

Spelling Strategies

Look, Say, Cover, Write, Check

Look at the word. Say the word.	Cover the word. Write out the word.	check

____

Spelling Strategies

Look, Say, Cover, Write, Check

Word	1st Try	2nd Try	3rd Try

Spelling Strategies

Memory Joggers

To help with keywords for upper KS2.

Teacher's Tips

Mnemonics or memory joggers can help spell trickier words. They are often used as a reminder for commonly used key words which are irregularly spelt. A memory jogger can be used to remember the whole word or just the tricky part. Try making up your own!

Word	Memory jogger
address	**add** your address
achieve	I know **Eve** can achieve.
business	Take a **bus** to your business.
competition	Did my **pet** win the competition?
difficulty	Mrs **D**, Mrs **I**, Mrs **FFI**, Mrs **C**, Mrs **U**, Mrs **LTY**.
definite	The fish's **fin** was definitely red.
dilemma	**Emma** has a dilemma.
enough	**E**nough **n**ow, **O**h **U** **G**reedy **H**ippo!
mosquito	Got to get the mos**quit**o to 'quit' biting me!

Spelling Strategies

Memory Joggers

hip/po/pot/am/us

necessary	Is it necessary to have **1 c**at and **2 s**nakes?
sandwich	Don't leave your sandwich on the **sand**.
secretary	The secretary had a **secret.**
separate	Look for 'a rat' in sep**arat**e
soldier	A soldier can **die** in action.
vegetable	I can get the ve**get**ables.
yacht	**Y**achts **a**nd **c**anoes **h**ate **t**hunderstorms.

Memory Joggers

address

Add your address.

achieve

I know Eve
can achieve.

business

Take the bus to
your business.

competition

Did my pet win the competition?

difficulty

Mrs D, Mrs I, Mrs FFI,

Mrs C, Mrs U, Mrs LTY.

definite

The fish's fin was definitely red!

Memory Joggers

dilemma

Emma has a dilemma.

enough

Enough now!

O U greedy hippo!

necessary

Is it necessary to have 1 cat and 2 snakes?

sandwich

Don't drop your sandwich on the sand.

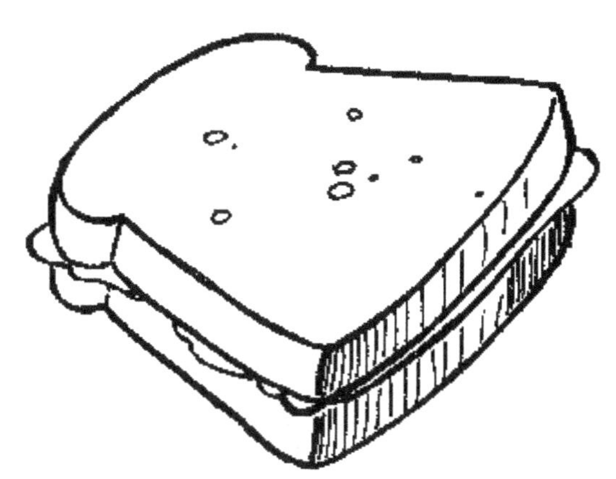

secretary

The secretary has a secret.

separate

Look out for 'a rat' in separate.

Memory Joggers

soldier

A soldier can die in action.

vegetable

I can get the vegetables.

yacht

Yachts and canoes hate thunderstorms.

Words Within Words

Many words have smaller words hiding within them. This can be a useful strategy to help spell a trickier word.

How many smaller words can you find in the following words?

temperament	something	furthermore
temper		
era		
ram		
men		
me		
amen		

pretending	grandmother	whatever

Underline the smaller words which appear within the longer word.

h <u>e a r</u> d	i l l e g a l	s o l d i e r
c h a r a c t e r	b e l i e v e	d e s p e r a t e
m a g n e t i c	e x p e n s i v e	b u s i n e s s
a p p e t i t e	f a v o u r i t e	e m b a r r a s s
i n f o r m a t i o n	c o n s o n a n t	f l a m b o y a n t

hip/po/pot/am/us

Spelling Strategies

Split Words into Syllables

Rules of Syllabification

Syllable breakdown exercises can really help with spelling and reading skills and encourage pupils not to contract words. When a longer word is split into syllables, it is broken down into little spoken chunks,
eg: **hip** / **po** / **pot** / **am** / **us**. Each chunk is called a syllable.

Focus on identifying the short and long vowel sounds.

Compound word syllable

Split between the two smaller words inside it.

For example:

saucepan	newspaper	earthworm
sauce / pan	news / paper	earth / worm

Open syllable

When the syllable ends in a long vowel sound: Vowel/Consonant/Vowel (VCV), and a single consonant comes between two vowels, we split the syllables before the consonant to keep the vowel long.
For example:

frequent	student	famous
fre / quent	stu / dent	fa / mous

Closed syllable

Closed syllables have a consonant, vowel, consonant (CVC) pattern and the vowel sound is short saying its sound. When a single consonant comes between the two vowels, we split after the consonant keeping the vowel short.
For example:

planet	camel	imagine
plan / et	cam / el	im / ag / ine

Spelling Strategies

Rules of Syllabification

Short vowel sound followed by two consonants (VCCV)

Split between the two consonants.
For example:

bargain	appear	aggressive
bar / gain	ap / pear	ag / gres / sive

If there is a short vowel sound followed by more than two consonants, split keeping the blends together.

For example:

monster	approve	dolphin
mon / ster	ap / prove	dol / phin

Consonant plus 'le' syllable

If a word ends in a consonant + le, split before the consonant. If there are two consonants + le split in between the consonants.

For example:

table	crumple	apple
ta / ble	crum / ple	ap / ple

'r' Combination

Split after ur, ar, ir
For example:

curtain,	target	circus
cur / tain	tar / get	cir / cus

REMEMBER

Split the prefixes and suffixes from the base or root word.
For example:

disappointment	protected
dis / ap / point / ment	pro / tect / ed

Every syllable has to have at least one vowel or part time vowel **'y'**.

Spelling Strategies

Identifying Unstressed Vowels in Syllables: /uh/, /eh/, /ih/ Sound

Some English words have unstressed vowels. Unstressed vowels are vowel sounds that are hard to hear when we say a word out loud. It can be helpful to mispronounce some words with unstressed vowels if need be, in order to spell the word correctly. For example cam/er/a, as opposed to what you often hear cam/ra which is an incorrect spelling. In this case, the unstressed vowel being a soft 'e' which is not normally defined in pronunciation, hence 'cam/ra'.

Check out these words with unstressed vowels.

int**e**rest	jewell**e**ry	cam**e**ra
libr**a**ry	prim**a**ry	secret**a**ry
gen**e**ral	comp**a**ny	diff**e**rent
fam**i**ly	valu**a**ble	pois**o**nous
bus**i**ness	def**i**nite	pref**e**rence
off**e**ring	desp**e**rate	prosp**e**rous
Wedn**e**sday	parli**a**ment	marv**e**llous
lit**e**racy	fact**o**ry	volunt**a**ry
int**e**rested	cath**o**lic	stationer**y**
mem**o**rable	temp**e**rature	math**e**matics
ref**e**rence	sep**a**rate	gen**e**rous

Many verbs have the stress on the second syllable. Look at these verbs where the second syllable is unstressed.

lim**i**ted	fast**e**ned	threat**e**ned
wid**e**ning	length**e**ned	deaf**e**ning
wond**e**ring	aband**o**ned	gard**e**ning
fatt**e**ning	strength**e**ning	fright**e**ning

Spelling Strategies

Identifying Unstressed Vowels

Root Words Ending in *'fer'*

refer	referred	referring	referral	reference

Say the word out loud!

If '**fer**' is not stressed – just add the suffix.

If '**fer**' is stressed – double the consonant before adding the suffix.

Circle the '**fer**' words that have unstressed vowels. (There are 4 to find!)

deferred	suffering	referral	preference	inference
referring		transferrable	offering	

Choose the correct word from the box to complete the sentences.

inference	deferred	offering	transferred	reference
referee	preferable	difference	conferred	

1. The ______________________ was in charge of the football match.
2. We had to look for ______________________ in the reading comprehension passage.
3. Encyclopaedias and dictionaries are ______________________ books.
4. Mint chocolate rather than plain chocolate is ______________________ for me.
5. Sports day will be ______________________ until next week because of heavy rain.
6. Have you ______________________ the money into your bank account?
7. Our team ______________________ together and came up with the right answer.
8. There was a big ______________________ in their height as one boy was much taller.
9. Mum is ______________________ to make cakes for the charity event.

Keywords

Keywords Learning Chart

Teacher's Tips

Words that the Department for Education (DFE) expects pupils to know how to spell by the age of 9 years.

accident (ally)	actual (ly)	address	answer	appear
arrive	believe	bicycle	breath	breathe
build	busy/ business	calendar	caught	centre
century	certain	circle	complete	consider
continue	decide	describe	different	difficult
disappear	early	earth	eight/ eighth	enough
exercise	experience	experiment	extreme	famous
favourite	February	forward(s)	fruit	grammar
group	guard	guide	heard	heart
height	history	imagine	increase	important
interest	island	knowledge	learn	length
library	material	medicine	mention	minute
natural	naughty	notice	occasion (ally)	often
opposite	ordinary	particular	peculiar	perhaps
popular	position	possess (ion)	possible	potatoes
pressure	probably	promise	purpose	quarter
question	recent	regular	reign	remember
sentence	separate	special	straight	strange
strength	suppose	surprise	therefore	through/ although
thought	through	various	weight	woman/ women

Department for Education 2013, *The National Curriculum in England.* **Reused under the terms of the Open Government License.**

Keywords Learning Chart

Words that the Department for Education (DFE) expects pupils to know how to spell by the age of 11 years.

accommodate	accompany	according	achieve	aggressive
amateur	ancient	apparent	appreciate	attached
available	average	awkward	bargain	bruise
category	cemetery	committee	communicate	community
competition	conscience	conscious	controversy	convenience
correspond	criticise	curiosity	definite	desperate
determined	develop	dictionary	disastrous	embarrass
environment	equip(ped/ment)	especially	exaggerate	excellent
existence	explanation	familiar	foreign	forty
frequently	government	guarantee	harass	hindrance
identity	immediate (ly)	individual	interfere	interrupt
language	leisure	lightning	marvellous	mischievous
muscle	necessary	neighbour	nuisance	occupy
occur	opportunity	parliament	persuade	physical
prejudice	privilege	profession	programme	pronunciation
queue	recognise	recommend	relevant	restaurant
rhyme	rhythm	sacrifice	secretary	shoulder
signature	sincere(ly)	soldier	stomach	sufficient
suggest	symbol	system	temperature	thorough
twelfth	variety	vegetable	vehicle	yacht

Department for Education 2013, ***The National Curriculum in England.*** **Reused under the terms of the Open Government License.**

Keywords

'-ough' Words

There are not many words with this 'ough' letter pattern but there are seven ways to pronounce the sound using the same letters!

/or/ /aw/	/uff/	/oh/	/ow/	/off/	/uh/	/oo/
bought	enough	dough	plough	cough	borough	through
brought	rough	though	bough	trough	thorough	
fought	tough	although	drought			
nought						
thought						

Fill in the gaps with the appropriate word from the boxes above.

1. Last week Sam had a heavy cold and a tickly ____________________ .
2. The cook rolled the ____________________ out to make some biscuits.
3. There was more than ____________________ food to eat at the banquet.
4. When you multiply ____________________ by ten you still get nought!
5. The soldiers ____________________ bravely in the battle to overcome the enemy.
6. The boat race had to be cancelled because of the ____________________ sea.
7. The horses drank from the water ____________________ in the field.
8. The lack of rain caused a severe ____________________ making the soil dry.

Find an '**ough**' word that rhymes with the words below.

fort nought	off	wart
slow	blue	cuff
cow	stuff	blow
sport	crow	scoff

Write a sentence with 'bought' (present tense buy).

____

Write a sentence with 'brought' (present tense bring).

____

changeable

Word Suffixes Basic Rules

A suffix is a letter or a group of letters which is added to the end of a word to form a new word.

Basic rules to follow:

Suffix	Guidelines	Examples
-able	We usually use '**-able**' when you hear the whole of the root word, but spellings may change depending on: if the word ends in '**e**' we drop the '**e**' and add '**-able**'. if the word ends in '**ce**' or '**ge**' we keep the '**e**' and add '**-able**'. or if a word ends in '**y**' we usually change the '**y**' to an '**i**' and add '**-able**'.	depend – dependable comfort – comfortable love – lovable believe – believable notice – noticeable change – changeable rely – reliable
-ible	We usually use '**-ible**' when the base word is incomplete. Common exceptions: flexible digestible, accessible.	impossible incredible

-ant **-ance**	'**-ant**', '**-ance**' is generally used to make '**c**' and '**g**' hard.	significant – significance extravagant – extravagance
-ancy	Used to form nouns from words ending '**-ant**'.	infant – infancy pregnant – pregnancy

Teacher's Tips

Suffixes

Word Suffixes Basic Rules

Suffix	Guidelines	Examples
-ary	Used often for adjectives.	imagine – imaginary extraordinary
-ery	Often added to a root word rather than an essential part of it.	bake – bakery nurse – nursery jewel – jewellery
-ory	Usually after the letter '**t**' or '**s**' Many words ending in '**-ory**' are related to words ending in '**-ion**'.	fact – factory introduction – introductory compulsion – compulsory
-ent	'**-ent**' '**-ence**' after a '**c**' or '**g**' is generally used to keep **c** and **g** soft.	innocent – innocence intelligent – intelligence
-ence	'**-ent**' '**-ence**' is generally used after 'qu'.	eloquent – eloquence
-ency	'**-ency** 'is used to form nouns from adjectives that end in '**-ent**'.	urgent– urgency consistent – consistency
-ify	'**-ify** ' is used to create verbs.	pure – purify simple – simplify
-ity	'**-ity**' is used to create nouns.	able – ability real – reality
-cial	Use '**-cial**' after a vowel . Exceptions: financial, commercial provincial	social official special
-tial	Use '**-tial**' after a consonant. Exceptions : initial, spatial, palatial	partial essential

Suffixes

'-able', '-ible' Words

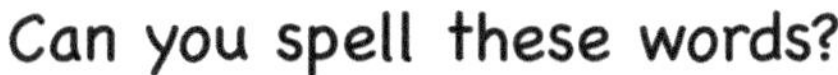
Can you spell these words?

Set A '-able'	Set B '-able'	Set A '-ible'	Set B '-ible'
unable	irritable	edible	illegible
capable	valuable	flexible	digestible
lovable	available	legible	incredible
reliable	vegetable	visible	impossible
probable	vunerable	eligible	divisible
washable	achievable	inedible	responsible
agreeable	unbelievable	possible	accessible
miserable	rechargeable	audible	irresistible
noticeable	irreplaceable	invisible	susceptible
changeable	knowledgeable	reversible	indestructible

Guidance	
Words ending in **'e'**	drop the **'e'** and add **'-able'** eg: love – lovable
Words ending in **'ce'** / **'ge'**	keep the **'e'** and add **'-able'** eg: noti**ce**able, chan**ge**able
Words ending in **'y'**	change **'y'** to **'i'** + add **'-able'** eg: vary – variable

Can you write some sentences using words from the table above?

1. ....

2. ....

3. ....

4. ....

5. ....

6. ....

Suffixes

'-able', '-ible' Words

Read the passage and highlight the words ending with the suffix **'-able'** and **'-ible'**.

Meg McGlible was a lovable lady who was an extremely capable nurse, providing medical assistance to people in the comfort of their own home. She played a valuable role in the community, because she was responsible for the welfare of several elderly people. They were a bit vulnerable, as they lived on their own, and all had issues with their health. It was unbelievable the time Meg spent helping others and it was impossible not to admire her efforts. However in spite of all the demands of her job, she always made time for her allotment. She was extremely knowledgeable about all aspects of gardening and especially loved growing fruit and vegetables. When she was not working, she often could be seen at her allotment. It was noticeable that her fruit and vegetables always looked bigger and better than those in the neighbouring allotments. After she had picked the produce, Meg spent time making a considerable number of fruit pies and different soups. She took some of this food to her older patients, who told her that her soups and pies were irresistible because they were so tasty to eat.

Can you split these words up into syllables? The first one has been done for you.

k n o w l e d g e a b l e	k n o w / l e d g e / a / b l e
u n b e l i e v a b l e	
i n d e s t r u c t i b l e	
u n e m p l o y a b l e	
i n c o m p r e h e n s i b l e	

Suffixes

changeable

'-able', '-ible' Words

Complete the words in the table below. Choose either '**-ible**' or '**-able**'.

Tip: We usually use the suffix '**-able**' when you hear the whole of the root word otherwise use the suffix '**-ible**'.

ador	sens	comfort	enjoy
reason	aud	terr	incred
depend	believ	charge	invis

Choose the correct word from the table below to complete the following sentences.

invisible	washable	disposable	possible	vegetable
comfortable	legible	unable	inedible	unbelievable

1. Carrots, turnips and parsnips are all root ______________________ s.
2. You must make your writing ______________________ so it is easy to read.
3. That jacket is not ______________________ ; it must go to the dry cleaners.
4. Harry Potter put on a magic coat and became ______________________ .
5. "Please can I have some ______________________ nappies?" said the young mother.
6. The vibrant colours used in that painting are ______________________ .
7. I am ______________________ to go out because I am not feeling well.
8. "Let's make sure we buy a ______________________ settee," said Dad.
9. It is ______________________ to see for miles from the top of that high tower.
10. The stew was ______________________ because the meat was tough.

Draw lines to match the word with its meaning.

Word	Meaning
vulnerable	trustworthy, dependable
edible	worth a lot
visible	unbelievable, hard to believe
reliable	at risk, helpless
incredible	suitable for eating
valuable	able to be seen

Suffixes

'-ant', '-ance', '-ancy' Words

Can you spell these words?

Set A	
'-ant', '-ance', '-ancy'	
distant	fragrance
pleasant	tolerance
fragrant	distance
ignorant	ignorance
abundant	arrogance
important	reluctancy
arrogant	tenancy
entrance	vacancy
importance	redundancy
performance	truancy

Set B	
'-ant', '-ance', '-ancy'	
brilliant	admittance
disinfectant	nuisance
restaurant	resistance
significant	assistance
descendant	allowance
extravagant	acquaintance
flamboyant	disappearance
ambulance	infancy
extravagance	buoyancy
significance	pregnancy

Guidance:
'**-ant**' or '**-ance**' is generally used to keep **c** and **g** hard eg, extravagant, significance.

Write a sentence using a word or words from Set A or Set B.

1. ....

2. ....

3. ....

4. ....

5. ....

6. ....

7. ....

8. ....

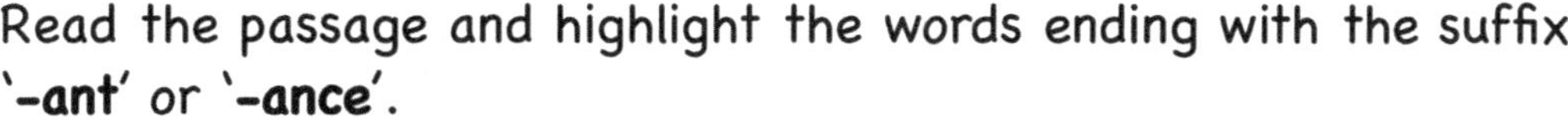

Suffixes

'-ant', '-ance', '-ancy' Words

Read the passage and highlight the words ending with the suffix '**-ant**' or '**-ance**'.

Constance Brown went out to lunch on Friday to a restaurant, called the 'White Elephant,' with an acquaintance from her work. She thought the entrance of the restaurant looked very ordinary, but she had a pleasant surprise when she went inside. The restaurant was decorated in a flamboyant style. The walls were painted in a rich peacock blue colour and on the back wall she noticed a striking painting of a sunset. A number of tall lush green plants had been elegantly placed around the room and a large vase full of beautiful red orchids filled the place with a lovely fragrance. The service was excellent and there was a constant flow of attendants at each dining table, who saw to it that the diners had everything that they needed. Constance was impressed by her choice from the menu. She had ordered a roast pheasant pie followed by a sponge cake filled with thick cream and blackcurrants for pudding. Her food was delicious and good value for money so she did not think the price was exorbitant. She had a brilliant time at the restaurant so she would not be at all hesitant to recommend the 'White Elephant' restaurant to all of her friends.

Can you split these words up into syllables?

reluctance	re/luc/tance
flamboyant	
extravagance	
exorbitancy	
insignificant	

Suffixes

'-ant', '-ance', '-ancy' Words

Choose the correct word from the table below to complete the following sentences.

entrance	restaurant	important	attendance	distant
disinfectant	annoyance	vacancy	redundancy	assistance

1. Our local restaurant has a ______________________ for a part-time chef.
2. Bleach is a strong ______________________ which is found in most households.
3. My dad took voluntary ______________________ as he was nearing retirement.
4. The ______________________ to the driveway was blocked by a car.
5. It is ______________________ to brush your teeth every day.
6. The teacher takes a register to mark her pupils' ______________________ .
7. Dad enjoyed the roast dinner he ate at the ______________________ .
8. Can I be of any ______________________ ?" asked the helpful porter.
9. Much to his ______________________ the children were making a lot of noise.
10. The Moon is very ______________________ from the Earth.

Make word family groups. Use '**-ant**' and '**-ance**' suffixes.

Tip: Drop '**e**' at the end of a word and add the vowel suffix.

		add ***-ant***	add ***-ance***
1	assist		
2	observe		
3	attend		
4	resist		
5	import		
6	ignore		
7	absorb		
8	expect		

Suffixes

'-ant', '-ance', '-ancy' Words

Match up the words in the box below with their meanings.

croissant	distant	flamboyant	abundance
buoyancy	extravagant	infancy	pleasant

1. Showy or brilliant in colour = ______________________
2. Ability to float on water = ______________________
3. The early stage in the development of something = ______________________
4. Far apart or far away = ______________________
5. Enjoyable or easy to like = ______________________
6. A great quantity = ______________________
7. Spending too much money = ______________________
8. A French, half-moon shaped pastry = ______________________

Pick four of these words and write an interesting sentence using each of the words showing you understand the meaning.

1. ____
2. ____
3. ____
4. ____

Write the root word for each of the words below.

observance	observe	resistant	
grievance		infancy	
inhabitant		allowance	

Suffixes

'-ent', '-ence', '-ency' Words

Can you spell these words?

Set A	
'-ent', '-ence', '-ency'	
talent	science
student	confidence
absent	difference
excellent	absence
frequent	sequence
accident	evidence
different	existence
continent	potency
confident	urgency
sentence	tendency

Set B	
'-ent', '-ence', '-ency'	
patient	experience
ancient	intelligence
intelligent	inconvenient
convenient	conscience
innocent	consequence
disobedient	convenience
magnificent	disobedience
innocence	emergency
patience	frequency
circumference	currency

Guidance:
'-ent' '-ence' is generally used to keep **'c'** soft eg: innocent, innocence
'-ent' '-ence' is generally used after **'qu'** eg: frequent, eloquence

Make sentences using a word or words from Set A or Set B.

1. ....

2. ....

3. ....

4. ....

5. ....

6. ....

Suffixes

'-ent', '-ence', '-ency' Words

Read the passage and highlight the words ending in **'-ent'** and **'-ence'**.

Priya Gil had just moved house and she wanted to make a difference to the place where she now lived. Her new home, which was surrounded by a wooden fence, had a small backyard but there was an absence of any plants or bushes or trees. Priya wanted to create a magnificent garden in the space, although she had not had any previous experience as a gardener. However, she did have a lot of persistence when faced with a challenge, as everybody who knew her would confirm. She had confidence in her abilities and also had the tendency to read books and research online to find out as much as she could about gardening. She put a lot of thought into the design of her new garden, gaining further inspiration from the frequency of her visits to different open gardens and displays. Her diligence paid off and she was delighted to discover, she had a real talent for gardening. Over the following weeks she managed to create a beautiful garden. Once it was finished she invited several of her friends to come and visit her. When they came round they were impressed by her beautiful garden and congratulated her on the magnificence of what was her back yard!

Can you split these words up into syllables?

e m e r g e n c y	e / m e r / g e n / c y
c o n v a l e s c e n t	
i n c o n v e n i e n t	
i n t e r d e p e n d e n c e	
c o n s i s t e n c y	
c o r r e s p o n d e n c e	

Suffixes

'-ent', '-ence', '-ency' Words

sentence	students	continent	president	currency
consequence	accident	evidence	urgency	absence

Choose the correct word from the box above to complete the sentences.

1. As a ______________________ of the drought, the soil is very dry.
2. The river Nile runs through the ______________________ of Africa.
3. There are many ______________________ studying in colleges and universities.
4. The girl's ______________________ was noted by the teacher.
5. The judge examined the ______________________ and then gave his verdict.
6. Do remember the capital letter and full stop in a ______________________ .
7. The ______________________ used in Japan is the 'yen'.
8. Mum has had an ______________________ and broken her leg.
9. Donald Trump was the ______________________ of the United States of America.
10. It was a matter of ______________________ to get the sick boy to hospital.

Complete the set.

Tip: Knock the '**t**' off the end of a word before adding **'-ence'** or **'-ency'**.

	-ence	**-ency**
dependent	dependence	dependency
frequent		
convenient		
lenient		
persistent		
impudent		

Suffixes

'-ent', '-ence', '-ency' Words

Match up the words in the box below with their meanings.

ancient	convenient	emergency	correspondence
convalescent	absence	frequent	difference

1. Fits in well, suitable = ____________________
2. Happening often = ____________________
3. Not the same = ____________________
4. Extremely old = ____________________
5. Letters and messages = ____________________
6. Not being present = ____________________
7. A recovering patient = ____________________
8. A serious situation = ____________________

Choose four of the words above and write an interesting sentence to show that you understand their meanings.

1. ____________________
2. ____________________
3. ____________________
4. ____________________

Write the root word for each of the words below.

fluency	fluent	confidence	
innocence		urgency	
frequency		disappearance	

Suffixes

'-ary', '-ery', '-ory' Words

Set A		
-ary	-ery	-ory
diary	bakery	story
library	lottery	ivory
primary	battery	victory
solitary	misery	factory
January	bravery	rectory
voluntary	nursery	history
ordinary	surgery	memory
dictionary	rockery	category
secondary	scenery	directory
temporary	recovery	territory

Set B		
-ary	-ery	-ory
voluntary	gallery	auditory
February	mystery	laboratory
legendary	grocery	accessory
necessary	slippery	dormitory
imaginary	delivery	predatory
stationary	discovery	satisfactory
vocabulary	celery	compulsory
anniversary	jewellery	introductory
complimentary	machinery	contradictory
	confectionery	conservatory

Guidance:

-ary Used often for adjectives.
-ery Often added to a root word rather than an essential part of it.
-ory Usually used after the letter 't' or 's'.

Suffixes

'-ary' Words

Read the passage and highlight the words ending in **'-ary'**.

Max Zachary moved back to England just before Christmas, after several years as a teacher in a missionary school in Africa. In January a secondary school in Kent employed him on a temporary basis. Max had a passion for English and inspired all his classes to write in a creative manner. First of all, he made the pupils think of an imaginary character in detail, and then he asked them to weave that person into an interesting story. He told all his students that it was necessary to extend their vocabulary in order to boost their literacy skills. Eager to gain his favour, many of his students could be seen in the school library with a dictionary at hand, to complete his homework tasks. Needless to say the headmaster was very complimentary to Max about his method of teaching, telling him he had raised the standard of English, in a most extraordinary way, throughout the whole school. Max was delighted when the Headmaster asked him to be a permanent member of staff rather than just a temporary worker. As an added bonus the Headmaster promoted him to Head of English at the school!

Can you split these words up into syllables?

v o c a b u l a r y	v o / c a b / u / l a r / y
a n n i v e r s a r y	
e x t r a o r d i n a r y	
i n t e r m e d i a r y	
c o m p l i m e n t a r y	

Suffixes

'-ery' Words

Read the passage and highlight the **'-ery'** words.

Bill Bannery made a pleasant discovery the other day when he spotted a new business had just opened in a nearby village near his house. It was called 'The Olde Tea Shop.' He looked through the window and glimpsed an amazing selection of cakes and tempting confectionary. He noticed that the place had its own bakery, so food was home baked on the premises rather than delivered by a delivery man. He decided to take his mother there for a treat. They sat outside in the garden at the back of the tea shop, which had a beautiful rockery, and admired the scenery. A friendly waitress came and put some china plates and white napkins stitched with embroidery down on the table. After that she brought silver cutlery, two cups of steaming hot coffee and a plateful of cakes. The cakes tasted delicious and Bill's mother told the owner, who was a rather whiskery artist called Jeffery, how much she had enjoyed the tea. As they were leaving, Jeffery encouraged them to have a look in his gallery, which was right next door to the tea shop. Bill and his mother did peek into the gallery and his mother bought a painting and also a little pottery pig which caught her eye.

Can you break these words down into syllables?

stationary	sta/tion/ar/y
skullduggery	
bewitchery	
confectionery	
ironmongery	

Suffixes

'-ory' Words

Read the passage and highlight the **'-ory'** words.

I can remember my aunt who was called Marjory with much affection. During the Second World War when she was a young woman, she worked in a factory producing munitions, such as bombs and bullets. She sometimes had to handle chemicals to assemble the bullets. Once she told me that the constant contact with a chemical called sulphur temporarily turned her skin and hair yellow, earning her the nickname 'canary girl'. After the war she became a teacher and she taught history at a local preparatory school. It was a boarding school and she was in charge of a dormitory of girls. I loved to go and stay with her in the holidays, as she always had an interesting story to tell me. It was extremely pleasant to curl up in an armchair in her huge conservatory, and chat to her. She always made sure that there was a plateful of snacks on the table which I found very satisfactory! I remember there was a beautiful large ivory elephant in that room. My aunt Marjory was a very superstitious person and she believed that elephant would bring her good luck, as long as it remained part of her household inventory.

Can you break these words down into syllables?

o b l i g a t o r y	o b / l i g / a t / o r / y
c o n s e r v a t o r y	
i n f l a m m a t o r y	
c o n t r a d i c t o r y	
u n s a t i s f a c t o r y	

Suffixes

'-ary', '-ery', '-ory' Words

Choose the correct word from the box to complete the sentences.

secondary	January	bakery	ivory	laboratory
rectory	greenery	dictionary	anniversary	jewellery

1. ______________________ is the month of the year before February.
2. A vicar might live in a house called a ______________________ .
3. Elephant tusks are made of ______________________ .
4. The smell of bread from the ______________________ made me hungry.
5. In springtime you can see a lot of ______________________ on the trees.
6. There are a lot of interesting words in a ______________________ .
7. After primary school, pupils will attend ______________________ school.
8. Scientists are working in the ______________________ to find a cure.
9. She cleaned the rings, bracelets and other items of ______________________ .
10. We will have a party to celebrate our silver wedding ______________________ .

Draw lines to match the word to its meaning.

Word	Meaning
inventory	required to do
compulsory	a room with many beds
crockery	a list of things
confectionary	dishes and bowls etc
solitary	an area of land
mystery	by yourself
territory	a puzzling event
dormitory	different kinds of sweets

'-ary', '-ery', '-ory' Words

The two words below often get confused.

- stationary: (means unmoving or at a standstill)
- stationery: (means writing materials such as pen, paper, etc)

Write a sentence for each word to show the correct meaning of each.

____

____

____

____

Tip: To remember which one is which:
Match the **'er'** in *paper* to the **'er'** in stationery!

Circle the correct spelling.

1.	histary	history	histery
2.	nursory	nursery	nursary
3.	Februery	Februory	February
4.	ordinary	ordinory	ordinery
5.	mystary	mystery	mystory
6.	introductary	introductory	introductery

Change each word below so that it ends in **'-ory'**.

fact	factory	direct	
predator		victor	
contradiction		compulsion	.

Suffixes

'-ify', '-ity' Words

Can you spell these words?

Set A		Set B	
-ity	**-ify**	**-ity**	**-ify**
unity	unify	scarcity	justify
ability	notify	possibility	clarify
quality	verify	popularity	specify
security	purify	curiosity	amplify
identity	petrify	familiarity	classify
majority	terrify	opportunity	identify
nativity	glorify	immortality	simplify
captivity	simplify	reliability	personify
stupidity	magnify	electricity	intensify
community	horrify	individuality	disqualify

Guidance:
'-ify' is used to create verbs, for example, *pure* to *purify* or *simple* to *simplify.*
'-ity' is used to create nouns, like *able* to *ability* or *real* to *reality.*

Write six sentences using some of the words from the table above.

1. ______________________________

2. ______________________________

3. ______________________________

4. ______________________________

5. ______________________________

6. ______________________________

Suffixes

'-ify', '-ity' Words

Read the passage and highlight the **'-ify'** and **'-ity'** words.

It was just six weeks to Christmas and Class 2 were busy organising their nativity play. They were very excited to have the opportunity to perform the play in the local village hall. There was a lot of activity in class as the children were writing the script for the play with the help of their teacher, Miss Banks. The majority of the pupils had got their parts, but there were still auditions for the role of Mary. Although a lot of the girls wanted to be Mary, Jill Vanity was finally picked. The teacher was able to justify giving her the part, as Jill had written some lovely words for Mary to say. Miss Banks realised Jill was able to identify with Mary and could amplify her voice so everyone could hear her clearly. Everything was coming together nicely because Miss Banks was able to intensify the time spent in rehearsal practice. Her only concern was that there seemed to be a scarcity of cribs to place Baby Jesus in. Luckily, one of the parents gained a lot of popularity, when he made a crib and delivered it promptly to Class 2. Everything was now set for the nativity play and the pupils were looking forward to performing it soon to their parents.

Can you break these words down into syllables?

d e x t e r i t y	d e x / t e r / i t / y
i n t e n s i f y	
d i s q u a l i f y	
p o s s i b i l i t y	
i n d i v i d u a l i t y	

Suffixes

'-ify', '-ity' Words

magnify	nativity	justify	agility
petrify	notify	electricity	qualify
opportunity	scarcity	amplify	captivity

Choose the correct word from the box above to complete the sentences.

1. My aunt always told me that spiders ______________________ her.
2. Class 2 will perform their ______________________ play in December.
3 We have the ______________________ to go to Spain this Easter.
4. The young gymnasts showed a lot of ______________________ on the bars.
5. Can you ______________________ that picture and make it bigger?
6. The kettle would not work as the ______________________ was turned off.
7. There is a ______________________ of flour in the shops right now!
8. Can you ______________________ spending all that money on clothes?
9. Tom wants to ______________________ for the swimming team.
10 The DJ will ______________________ the music so everybody can hear it.
11 You have to ______________________ the school if you are going to be absent.
12 Is it cruel to keep animals in ______________________ in cages?

Add **'-ify'** or **'-ity'** to these partial words. Can you add both?

> **Tip: '-ify'** words are usually verbs and **'-ity'** words are usually nouns.

not**ify**	celebr	grav	magn
qual	horr	ident	glor

Draw lines to match the word to its meaning.

Word	Meaning
specify	a lack of something
unify	to state or identify clearly
amplify	the most of something
scarcity	to become united
dexterity	a skill in physical movement
majority	to increase the volume of

'-cial', '-tial' Words

Can you spell these words?

Set A		Set B	
'-cial'	**'-tial'**	**'-cial'**	**'-tial'**
facial	initial	official	sequential
racial	partial	artificial	celestial
social	palatial	beneficial	residential
glacial	potential	commercial	influential
crucial	essential	superficial	substantial
special	impartial	sacrificial	unessential
financial	torrential	unofficial	presidential
antisocial	confidential	provincial	preferential

Guidance

Use **'-cial'** after a vowel. (Exceptions: financial, commercial, provincial)
Use **'-tial'** after a consonant. (Exceptions: initial, palatial.)

Choose six words from the box above and write a sentence for each.

1. ____________________

2. ____________________

3. ____________________

4. ____________________

5. ____________________

6. ____________________

Suffixes

'-cial', '-tial' Words

Read the passage and highlight the **'-cial'** and **'-tial'** words.

I had seen from various television broadcasts that torrential rain had caused massive flooding in South Africa, in an area where I had originally lived. My initial reaction to the damage wrecked by the storm was a feeling of horror. Most of the residential properties built near the river were half submerged in water. The situation had the potential to turn into a huge catastrophe, as so many people were badly affected. It was crucial that many of the townships received some kind of financial aid. Many of the inhabitants in the area had suffered severe destruction to their livelihood as their homes and crops were destroyed.

I was relieved to learn today, in an update on this news, that help was at hand. It was a big relief to me that a benefactor, who was an influential entrepreneur, had kindly contributed a large cash sum of money to the rescue fund, which had been set up to help the people in the various settlements. I know that all these communities would be so grateful to receive this special financial aid as it would enable them to rebuild their homes as soon as the flooding had subsided.

Can you break these words down into syllables?

confidential	con/fid/en/tial
commercial	
provincial	
unsubstantial	
quintessential	

Suffixes

'-cial', '-tial' Words

Choose the correct word from the box to complete the sentences.

initial	special	palatial	confidential	antisocial
artificial	potential	torrential	commercial	unessential

1. Those flowers are not real, they are ______________________ .
2. The house was like a grand palace, it was so big and ______________________ .
3. He had the ______________________ to become a great musician.
4. Do not tell anyone this news because it is ______________________ .
5. The ______________________ rain caused the river to flood its banks.
6. The ______________________ meeting was held last Tuesday.
7. The little boy really hoped to get a ______________________ treat.
8. He is rude and unfriendly so he is an ______________________ person.
9. Something that is not necessary is ______________________ .
10. Did you watch that ______________________ on the television?

Draw lines to match the word to its meaning.

Word	Meaning
quintessential →	the most perfect
special	looking like a palace
potential	really important
palatial	something private and secret
crucial	something extraordinary
confidential	an ability that can be developed

Add **'-tial'** or **'-cial'** word endings to these partial words.

Tip: Usually **'-tial'** comes after a consonant and **'-cial'** usually after a vowel.

fa	gla	antiso	cru
residen	offi	spe	substan
influen	mar	celes	poten

Dictation Exercises

Suffixes

> **NOTE:** Target words are underlined.
> Emphasize the words in *italics*.
> Sentences in **bold** are harder dictation.

'-able'

1. I am *often* unable to come out and play.
2. We had an enjoyable day at the seaside.
3. My mother did not think the silk jacket was washable.
4. It is probable Gran will not *remember* to post the letter.
5. **The man was incapable of *building* up the *business*.**
6. **The vegetable garden was at the front of the house.**
7. **"I will be available to play for the team in *February*," said Bill.**
8. **He decided to buy the armchair because it was comfortable.**

'-ible'

1. It is not possible that bread is edible!
2. The *island* was not visible because of the mist.
3. If something is invisible it cannot be seen.
4. "Please make your handwriting legible," said the teacher.
5. **It was impossible to cross the channel in the storm.**
6. **I *believe* my sister was responsible for all the mess!**
7. **If something is indestructible is it *difficult* to break?**
8. **My brother is susceptible to hay fever when the pollen count is high.**

'-able' and '-ible'

It was despicable that the elderly Mrs Brown had been robbed. She was having an enjoyable holiday with her cousin when a valuable ring was taken from her hotel room. She was *desperate* to recover it and hoped the *individual* responsible for the theft would soon be discovered.

'-ant'

1. The infant child made a lot of noise in the pram.
2. The flowers in the garden had a fragrant smell.
3. The boy gained brilliant marks in all of his exams.
4. I *notice* there is an abundant crop of plums this year.
5. **It is important to put some disinfectant down the sink.**
6. **My friend was extravagant and spent lots of money.**
7. **I *heard* the infant child making a lot of noise in the pram.**
8. **I don't know why there was such a *queue* to get into the restaurant.**

Dictation Exercises

Suffixes

> **NOTE:** Target words are underlined.
> Emphasize the words in *italics*.
> Sentences in **bold** are harder dictation.

'-ance'

1. The entrance to the road was blocked.
2. It is a short distance from my house to the shops.
3. There was a *beautiful* fragrance coming from the flowers.
4. Pat needs a lot of tolerance to cope with the frisky dog.
5. **To her annoyance, the man kept on making noise.**
6. **"Can I be of assistance?" said the helpful *guide* to Tom.**
7. **It is such an extravagance to spend that much money on a car!**
8. **The disappearance of my *neighbour's* cat caused a lot of concern.**

'-ant' and '-ance'

The cook at the restaurant had an abundance of flour in the cupboard. He was not hesitant to use it to make *forty different* bread rolls. It was a brilliant idea as the fragrant smell of the bread attracted a *queue* of customers. The owner had to have assistance to take all the orders!

'-ent'

1. The student hopes that he will pass all of his exams.
2. I am confident that they will do a good job.
3. He thinks that there is an excellent market in the town.
4. After the accident, my mum was looked after by a nurse.
5. **The ancient Romans knew how to build good roads.**
6. **The patient is coming home from hospital next week.**
7. **The disobedient boy was told off by his mother.**
8. **It is not convenient for my *neighbour* to go to the garden *centre*.**

'-ence'

1. A big silence fell as the boys were told the sad news.
2. Asif's absence from school was because of his illness.
3. "Please write in a full sentence," said the teacher.
4. There was no evidence to show he had stolen the car.
5. **She was running out of patience with the demanding child.**
6. **She knew that the man had yet to prove his innocence.**
7. **As a consequence of the frost, many plants did not survive.**
8. **Tom was surprised that the local convenience store stayed open late.**

Dictation Exercises

Suffixes

NOTE: Target words are underlined.
Emphasize the words in *italics*.
Sentences in **bold** are harder dictation.

'-ent' and '-ence' Words

In his *address*, the president of the college said that it was urgent that all the students worked hard. There might be a grim consequence if anyone *thought* that this would be inconvenient! He reminded the students that their diligence and persistence would be rewarded by good grades.

'-ary'

1. There was a black van in the library car park.
2. The diary was found hidden at the back of the chest.
3. The month of February comes before March in the year.
4. She is going to secondary school this September.
5. **He helped in the shop every Tuesday on a voluntary basis.**
6. **"It is necessary to pack up all your *favourite* toys," said mum.**
7. **I *thought* there was a glossary of words at the back of the book.**
8. **We were all given a complimentary ticket to see the show.**

'-ery'

1. There were a lot of alpine flowers in the rockery.
2. Sally *heard* that she had won the lottery on Friday!
3. Nadia could smell the freshly baked cakes in the bakery.
4. Spoons, forks and knives are all items of cutlery.
5. **The *soldier* made a rapid recovery from his illness.**
6. **Mum chopped up the celery into pieces to have in a salad.**
7. **The delivery van was crammed with *beautiful* flowers and *vegetables*.**
8. **I bought my gold ring from the jewellery shop in the High Street.**

'-ory'

1. Are the *elephant's* tusks made of ivory?
2. Jack wrote his history homework in a notebook.
3. The *woman* got a cake in the shop near the factory.
4. Dad *thought* the number would be in the directory.
5. **The *young* girl was fast asleep in the dormitory.**
6. **Is it compulsory to stay indoors if you have a virus?**
7. **The rats in the laboratory were part of an experiment.**
8. **The hen was not satisfactory because it did not lay any eggs.**

Dictation Exercises

Suffixes

NOTE: Target words are underlined.
Emphasize the words in *italics*.
Sentences in **bold** are harder dictation.

'-ary', '-ery' and '-ory' Words

It is necessary to keep stock of books by taking an inventory. If this is done to a satisfactory standard, books should not go missing. "It is important to remember not to eat confectionery when reading a book as it could make the pages sticky," said Miss Page, a library helper.

'-cial'

1. She would get a special present today.
2. It is crucial to revise for all your exams.
3. It is not easy to book a facial at that *popular* salon.
4. Letting your dog poop on the pavement is antisocial.
5. **The cut was not deep; it was just a superficial graze.**
6. **The commercial on the TV was about home insurance.**
7. **The nurse put the artificial flowers in the vase.**
8. **The victims of the flooding might need some financial aid.**

'-tial'

1. My Grandad is partial to a piece of cake.
2. "It is essential to get wellington boots," said Dad.
3. My initial reaction was *surprise* that he had won the cup.
4. I don't *suppose* the torrential rain damaged the crop.
5. **He got preferential treatment and went to the front of the *queue*.**
6. **My parents have been the most influential people in my life.**
7. **There is a substantial amount of *interest* in the project.**
8. **A lot of houses can be found in a residential area.**

'-cial' and '-tial'

We have some special news, but it is confidential so do not tell anybody else. A *familiar* influential person is giving us some financial aid. He is going to invest a substantial amount of money in our project which means we can carry on with our *experiment* on the *island*.

Dictation Exercises

Suffixes

> **NOTE:** Target words are underlined.
> Emphasize the words in *italics*.
> Sentences in **bold** are harder dictation.

'-ify'

1. Can you magnify the words on that note?
2. The man asked us to verify our *address*.
3. We will notify you if we hear anything.
4. Bill will not let the mad cat terrify him!
5. **I do hope the judge will not disqualify that rider.**
6. **You need to amplify the music so everyone can hear.**
7. **I cannot justify spending so much time in the shop.**
8. **He was not able to specify how much *medicine* he needed.**

'-ity'

1. I like to buy top quality plums from the shop.
2. The nativity play was held in the village hall.
3. There was much fun and jollity at the funfair.
4. Did I *mention* that gravity holds the planets in orbit?
5. **He was *certain* that he had the ability to go all the way.**
6. **I would like to take this opportunity to thank you for your help.**
7. **Is there a possibility that you could do my shopping today?**
8. **There was tight security on the pop star's *yacht*.**

'-ify' and '-ity'

I would like to take this opportunity to clarify the golf club's position. The majority of members are against the construction of a high speed train line as this will force the club to close. The project has little popularity with local people. I am *certain* the whole community will unify to try to stop it.

Functions of Suffixes

Changing Tense: Adding '-s/-es', '-ed' and '-ing'

1. With most verbs you just add '**-s**'/'**-es**', '**-ed**' or '**-ing**' to indicate tenses unless they are irregular verbs, such as: know/ knew or send/ sent etc.

HOWEVER

2. If a word ends in '**ch**,' '**sh**', '**ss**' or '**x**' you add '-**es**' when making the present tense. For example:

search	searches	bench	benches
wash	washes	crash	crashes
kiss	kisses	class	classes
mix	mixes	hoax	hoaxes

3. If a single syllable word ends in a '**short vowel** plus **consonant**' you DOUBLE the final consonant before adding '**-ing**' or '**-ed**'. For example:

plan	pla**nn**ing	pla**nn**ed
shop	sho**pp**ed	sho**pp**ing

4. If a word ends in an '**e**' drop the '**e**' before adding '**-es**', '**-ed**' or '**-ing**'. For example:

live	liv**es**	liv**ed**	liv**ing**
hope	hop**es**	hop**ed**	hop**ing**

5. If a word ends in a 'consonant plus **y**' – change '**y**' to '**i**' then add ending unless adding '**-ing**'. For example:

dry	dr**ies**	dr**ied**	dry**ing**
carry	carr**ies**	carr**ied**	carry**ing**

See Suffix Spelling Rule section p97–112 for more information.

Functions of Suffixes

Changing Tense: Adding '-s/-es', '-ed' and '-ing'

Complete the table.

	Verb	Present Tense **-s/-es**	Past Tense **-ed**	Present Participle **-ing**
1	jump	jumps	jumped	jumping
2	help			
3	hope	hopes		
4	stop		stopped	
5	try			
6	skip			
7	help			
8	wipe			
9	jog			
10	cry			
11	plan			
12	vary			varying
13	drag			
14	reply			
15	shout			
16	snatch			
17	supply			

Functions of Suffixes

Changing Tense: Adding '-ed' Word Endings

Remember the rules!
Circle the verbs, then rewrite the sentences changing them into the past tense.

1. The cat escapes into the garden.

2. I hurry down the road to the supermarket.

3. The large red balloon pops at the fete.

4. I am hoping to go for a swim after school today.

5. Dad will empty all the water from the paddling pool.

6. My brother jogs to the top of the road every day.

7. The clothes dry quickly on the washing line.

8. The burglar grabs a sack and stuffs in the jewellery.

9. Ella is whispering a secret to her friend.

10. He will carry all of the suitcases to the car.

11. When Sam travels to Australia, he will stop off in Thailand.

Functions of Suffixes

Changing Tense: Adding '-ed' and '-ing'

Complete the sentence using the correct tense of the verb in brackets.

1. After the party mum ______________________ in the chair. (relax)
2. Mark found a mouse ______________________ in the straw. (hide)
3. She ______________________ the heavy suitcase from under the bed. (drag)
4. Next week we are all ______________________ to America. (fly)
5. Are you ______________________ to watch our school play? (come)
6. Mum is busy in the garden ______________________ the hedge. (cut)
7. I ______________________ hard to get good marks in the exam. (try)
8. I like ______________________ in the park at the weekend. (cycle)
9. Have you ______________________ out of those dirty clothes? (change)
10. The little boy is ______________________ because he has lost his toy. (cry)

The paragraph below is written in the present tense. Change all the underlined words into the past tense. (Note there are some irregular past tense verbs.)

All of a sudden Ellie [1]hears a loud knock at the front door. When she [2]opens it there [3]isn't anybody there, but on the doorstep she [4]notices a large present with her name on it. Carefully she [5]will carry it into the lounge and [6]unwraps it quickly. She [7]grins when she [8]sees what [9]is inside.

1. ....
2. ....
3. ....
4. ....
5. ....
6. ....
7. ....
8. ....
9. ....

Functions of Suffixes

Changing Parts of Speech

Suffixes can change parts of speech. For example adding the suffix **'-ate'** changes the noun **pollen** into the verb **pollinate**.

Guidance:

When adding suffixes, for most words you just add the suffix.

If the root word ends in **'e'** or **'y'**, – remove the **'e'** or **'y'** before adding the suffix (except suffix **'-ment'**).

If adding **'-ness'** to words ending in **'y'** – change **'y'** to **'i'** before adding suffix **'-ness'**.

If adding **'-ate'** to words ending in **'-tion'**, remove **'-tion'** from the word and then add **'-ate'**.

Teacher's Tips

Changing nouns into verbs: Adding suffixes **'-ate'**, **'-en'**, **'-ify'** or **'-ise'**.

Noun	Verb	Noun	Verb
fabric	fabric**ate**	strength	strength**en**
vaccine	vaccin**ate**	sick	sick**en**
alien	alien**ate**	note	not**ify**
passion	passion**ate**	class	class**ify**
hyphen	hyphen**ate**	terror	terr**ify**
irritation	irrit**ate**	horror	horr**ify**
migration	migr**ate**	identity	ident**ify**
navigation	navig**ate**	final	final**ise**
light	light**en**	symbol	symbol**ise**
dark	dark**en**	apology	apolog**ise**
sweet	sweet**en**	sympathy	sympath**ise**
fright	fright**en**	fantasy	fantas**ise**
height	height**en**	advert	advert**ise**
length	length**en**	vandal	vandal**ise**

Functions of Suffixes

Changing Parts of Speech

Suffixes can change parts of speech. For example adding the suffix **'-ate'** changes the noun **pollen** into the verb **pollinate**.

Changing adjectives into nouns: Adding suffixes **'-ity'** or**'-ness'**.

Adjective	Noun	Adjective	Noun
rare	rar**ity**	intense	intens**ity**
agile	agil**ity**	responsible	responsibil**ity**
curious	curios**ity**	mad	mad**ness**
mature	matur**ity**	sad	sad**ness**
active	activ**ity**	slow	slow**ness**
stupid	stupid**ity**	kind	kind**ness**
weak	weak**ness**	dark	dark**ness**
hard	hard**ness**	happy	happi**ness**
soft	soft**ness**	empty	empti**ness**

Changing verbs into nouns: Adding suffixes **'-ance'**, **'-ment'**, **'-tion'**, **'-ation.**

Verb	Noun	Verb	Noun
rely	reli**ance**	amaze	amaze**ment**
accept	accept**ance**	excite	excite**ment**
admit	admitt**ance**	resent	resent**ment**
annoy	annoy**ance**	amuse	amuse**ment**
attend	attend**ance**	disappoint	disappoint**ment**
perform	perform**ance**	create	crea**tion**
reassure	reassur**ance**	collect	collec**tion**
observe	observ**ance**	migrate	migra**tion**
resemble	resembl**ance**	educate	educa**tion**
amuse	amuse**ment**	irritate	irrita**tion**
pay	pay**ment**	operate	opera**tion**
enjoy	enjoy**ment**	imagine	imagin**ation**
move	move**ment**	inform	inform**ation**
argue	argu**ment**	invite	invit**ation**
improve	improve**ment**	direct	direc**tion**

Functions of Suffixes

Changing Parts of Speech

Changing nouns into adjectives: Adding suffixes **'-y'**, **'-ful'**, '**-ous'** or **'-ly'**.

Noun	Adjective	Noun	Adjective
fluff	fluff**y**	delight	delight**ful**
dust	dust**y**	beauty	beauti**ful**
mess	mess**y**	colour	colour**ful**
greed	greed**y**	fame	fam**ous**
luck	luck**y**	fury	furi**ous**
spice	spic**y**	nerve	nerv**ous**
chill	chill**y**	poison	poison**ous**
sleep	sleep**y**	envy	envi**ous**
juice	juic**y**	venom	venom**ous**
health	health**y**	danger	danger**ous**
wealth	wealth**y**	mystery	mysteri**ous**
care	care**ful**	mountain	mountain**ous**
play	play**ful**	dead	dead**ly**
help	help**ful**	love	love**ly**
fear	fear**ful**	home	home**ly**
pain	pain**ful**	ghost	ghost**ly**
play	play**ful**	beast	beast**ly**
taste	taste**ful**	coward	coward**ly**
peace	peace**ful**	heaven	heaven**ly**
power	power**ful**	miser	miser**ly**
thought	thought**ful**	wool	wool**ly**

Show me activity

Ask the pupils to change a noun into an adjective or a noun /adjective into a verb etc on their individual whiteboards. Check then encourage them to use the word in a sentence.

Functions of Suffixes

Changing Parts of Speech

Suffixes can change parts of speech. Nouns, verbs and adjectives are formed from each other.

Write the verb for the noun.

action	**act**	drawing	
invitation		departure	
injury		security	
laughter		marriage	
movement		assistance	
annoyance		decoration	

Complete the sentences by changing the noun in the brackets to an adjective

Use the suffixes **'-y' '-ful' '-ous'**.

1. He was a ______________________ man to win the lottery. (luck)
2. It was a ______________________ red rose that she picked. (beauty)
3. It is ______________________ to run in the corridors. (danger)
4. Jack's ______________________ toe was throbbing a lot. (pain)
5. The ______________________ man counted his sacks of gold. (wealth)
6. The ______________________ pop star ran on to the stage. (fame)
7. She was ______________________ to make the old lady a cake. (thought)
8. It can be very ______________________ in the winter. (chill)
9. The coach was ______________________ that his team had lost. (fury)
10. The rash was making my skin feel very ______________________ . (itch)

Make an adjective from each of these nouns.

fluff	a	cat	trick	a	problem
poison	a	snake	power	a	engine
friend	a	face	love	a	smile
help	a	nurse	nerve	a	driver

Functions of Suffixes

Changing Parts of Speech

Sort the adjectives, nouns and verbs into the correct boxes.

alien	terror	curious	happiness	operate
thoughtful	imagination	greedy	cowardly	equalise
strengthen	apologise	gold	beautiful	frighten

	Nouns	Adjectives	Verbs
1			
2			
3			
4			
5			

Change the nouns into verbs.

Add the correct suffix for the noun in brackets and then complete the sentence. Remember nouns often use '**-ate**', '**-ise**' or '**-en**' to make them into verbs.

1 We can all ______________________ with the loss of your beloved pet. (sympathy)

2. I will close the curtains in order to ______________________ the room. (dark)

3. The nurse will ______________________ the children against small pox. (vaccine)

4. Please can you add more sugar to ______________________ my cup of tea. (sweet)

5. Tom needs to ______________________ for being so rude to his uncle. (apology)

6. He did not want to ______________________ his friends by not sharing his sweets. (alien)

7. The local shop will have to ______________________ for a paper boy. (advert)

8. Lucy put on a ______________________ jumper because she was cold. (wool)

Functions of Suffixes

Changing Parts of Speech

Change the adjectives and verbs into nouns.

Put the correct ending on the adjective or verb in brackets and then complete the sentence. Remember adjectives often use '**-ness**' or '**-ity**' and verbs can use '**-ment**' to make nouns.

1. The ______________________ of the bed gave me backache. (hard)
2. They had an ______________________ about who should do the washing up. (argue)
3. My sister has the ______________________ to do really well in the exams. (capable)
4. He was overwhelmed by the ______________________ he received after his accident. (kind)
5. I hope Dad will enjoy his ______________________ now he has finished working. (retire)
6. Tom's ______________________ at winning the race was plain for all to see. (happy)
7. I am sure that the boy's broken leg will limit his ______________________ . (mobile)
8. She watched in ______________________ as the magician performed the trick. (amaze)
9. We had no ______________________ when there was a power strike. (electric)
10. The ______________________ of the bed made it very comfortable. (soft)
11. To his great ______________________ the holiday had to be cancelled. (disappoint)
12. It was nice to have some ______________________ when the noisy music stopped. (quiet)

Prefixes

Prefixes are sets of letters that are added to the beginning of a word to alter the meaning of the word. They are not words in their own right and cannot stand on their own. Look at some of the most popular prefixes below and their meanings.

Prefix	Meaning	Examples
anti-	against	antisocial, antifreeze, antibiotic
auto-	self, own	autopilot, automatic, autobiography
bi-	two	bicycle, binoculars, bipolar
dis-	not, opposite	disobey, disappear, dishonest
ex-	out of	exit, exclude, export, expel
inter-	between	internet, interval, interrupt
mis-	wrongly	misused, mistreated, misfortune
non-	not	nonsense, non-fiction, non-stick
pre-	before	prehistoric, preview, predict
pro-	for, go forward	promote, proceed, procession
re-	again, back	repay, recede, reflect, repaint
sub-	under	subway, submarine, submerge
super-	above	supermarket, superstar, supersonic
tele-	over a distance	telephone, television, telescope
trans-	across	transfer, transport, transatlantic
un-	not	undo, unwrap, unwilling
uni-	one	unicorn, unicycle, uniform

Prefixes

'anti-', 'inter-', 'mis-', 'sub-', 'trans-' Words

anti- (against)	inter- (between)	mis- (wrongly)
antidote	interact	misjudge
antibody	internet	misspell
antisocial	interval	mistreat
antifreeze	interrupt	mistaken
antiseptic	interfere	misplaced
anticipate	interview	misconduct
antibacterial	interrogate	misfortune
antihistamine	intermission	misinterpret
antibiotics	intermittently	misunderstood
anticlimax	international	misbehaviour

sub- (under)	trans- (across)
subtract	transport
subdued	translate
suburbs	transferral
submerge	transaction
subsiding	transfusion
subscription	transferred
substitution	transatlantic
subconscious	transformation

Prefixes

'anti-', 'inter-', 'mis-', 'sub-', 'trans-' Words

Read the passage and highlight the prefix words **'anti-'**, **'inter-'**, **'mis-'**, **'sub-'** and **'trans-'**.

In the suburbs of Iquitos city in Peru, the English botanist Adam Frost had just set off to the Amazon Rainforest with a guide. He was extremely interested to find a rare flower called the Translucent Orchid. However, just at the start of the trek, he had the misfortune to be bitten by a Black Widow spider. Adam felt a substantial pain and then his leg became red and swollen. He misjudged the situation as he did not think it was necessary to go to the hospital. It was fortunate that his guide, Dylan Leon realised that it was important to transfer him quickly to the nearest hospital before the infection really took hold. Dylan also kindly acted as a translator when the Peruvian doctor, who could not speak English, asked Adam questions about what had happened. The doctor anticipated that Adam would get increasingly unwell and knew exactly what to do. He gave Adam a large shot of antihistamine, which proved to be the antidote to the venom from the spider's bite. Although the expedition was interrupted a short while, I can report that Adam did eventually find the rare Translucent Orchid in the Amazon Rainforest!

Can you split these words into syllables?

transformation	trans/form/a/tion
intermittently	
antihistamine	
intermediary	
misunderstanding	

Prefixes

'trans-', 'inter-' Words

Prefixes are sets of letters that are added to the beginning of a word and alter the meaning of the root or base word. They are not words in their own right and cannot stand on their own.

trans
The prefix **'trans-'** means across or other side of

inter
The prefix **'inter-'** means between or among

Draw lines to match the word to its meaning.

Word	Meaning
interval →	a period between two events or times
transcontinental	allowing light to pass through
transparent	to send from one place to another
interfere	to change from one thing into another
transmit	going across a continent
interrupt	to stop someone from speaking briefly
transform	to do things with others
interact	to take part in concerns of others

Fill in the blanks using the correct word from the table above.

1. Don't you think it's rude to ______________________ a conversation.
2. In the ______________________ in the show, we got out of our seats.
3. A ______________________ journey goes from one side of a continent to another.
4. The yachtsman promised to ______________________ messages every week.
5. Glass is usually ______________________ so you can see through it.
6. Don't ______________________ in what she is doing or there will be trouble.

Prefixes

'trans-', 'inter-' Words

Add either **'inter-'** or **'trans-'** to complete the sentences below.

1. The editor ____________lated a page of the letter from French into English.
2. I am asking you nicely not to ____________fere in their business.
3. My uncle took a ____________atlantic flight to New York yesterday.
4. Another name for the world wide web is the ____________net.
5. Tom had to have a blood ____________fusion when he was in hospital.
6. She had to have an ____________view before she got the job in the café.
7. The new hairstyle ____________formed my friend's appearance.
8. It is rude to ____________rupt when someone is talking.

Add the prefix **'inter-'** or **'trans-'** to complete the words.

late	val	ference
ruption	mit	port
form	national	parent
twine	viewer	fusion

Choose four words from the box and use each one to write an interesting sentence.

1. ____
2. ____
3. ____
4. ____

Prefixes

'anti-', 'mis-', 'sub-' Words

Prefixes are sets of letters that are added to the beginning of a word and alter the meaning of the word. They are not words in their own right and cannot stand on their own.

anti	mis	sub
The prefix **'anti-'** means against	The prefix **'mis-'** means wrongly	The prefix **'sub-'** means under

Draw lines to match the word to its meaning.

Word	Meaning
antihistamine	a ship that can travel underwater
misplaced	a drug that treats an allergy
antidote	rude or improper behaviour
submarine	put in the wrong place
subterranean	medicine that acts against poison
misbehaviour	underground, under the Earth's surface

Fill in the blanks with the correct word from above.

1. The boy's ______________________ in class earned him a punishment.
2. There is no known ______________________ to the poison of this spider!
3. The pollen made me sneeze, so I took an ______________________ tablet.
4. Gran has ______________________ her glasses; she can't find them anywhere.
5. There are lots of ______________________ tunnels in London.
6. The ______________________ submerged under the water to avoid the enemy ship.

Prefixes

Latin Numeral Prefixes

Memorising number prefixes will help you work out what new words mean.

Draw lines to match the word to its meaning.

Word	Meaning
trident	a ninety year old
unicorn	occurring every three years
octagon	one world
quintet	to multiply something by four
nonagenarian	imaginary horse with a long horn on its forehead
decade	eight sided shape
triennial	two legged animal
quadruple	a three pronged spear
universe	period of ten years
biped	a group of five singers

Reassemble the syllables in the correct order. Remember to find the number prefix first!

Syllables	Word
t o p s / c e / r a / t r i	t r i c e r a t o p s
s e p t / l e t s / u p	
o / b i / g r a p h / y	
p e d e / i / c e n t	
g l e / t r i / a n	

Prefixes

Latin Numeral Prefixes

Complete the sentences by choosing the correct word from the box below.

unicycle	binoculars	trilingual	quarters
million	universe	triangle	quadruplets

1. The clown rode a ______________________ at the circus.
2. Adil cut the apple carefully into ______________________.
3. There are many planets in the ______________________.
4. He looked through the ______________________ and saw the bird.
5. A ______________________ is the word used for a three sided shape.
6. She was ______________________ as she could speak French, German and Spanish.
7. If I won a ______________________ pounds I would be a millionaire.
8. Even though I have known Evie, Jade, Sadie and Josie for two years now, I still have trouble telling the ______________________ apart!

Can you find a word starting with either 'uni', 'bi' or 'tri' to fill in the blanks?

1. The country was ______________________ in grief when the Queen died.
2. It was a ______________________ experience when I swam with dolphins.
3. What a disaster! I managed to get punctures in both wheels of my ______________________.
4. My uncle was competing in his fourth ______________________, he has always excelled at swimming, cycling and running.
5. My sister bought me The Lord of the Rings ______________________. It will take a while to watch the three films.
6. With my mum being French and my dad English, my two brothers and I are ______________________. It's great speaking two languages!

Prefixes

Prefix Splits

Add a prefix to complete the words in the table below. Choose from these common prefixes.

anti-	auto-	bi-	ex-	dis-	inter-	mis-
non-	pre-	re-	sub-	super-	trans-	un-

1	sense	21	dict
2	clockwise	22	graph
3	market	23	understand
4	take	24	paint
5	mit	25	way
6	rupt	26	it
7	marine	27	sonic
8	vision	28	lucky
9	matic	29	lax
10	pel	30	septic
11	appear	31	cord
12	net	32	willing
13	treat	33	fer
14	kind	34	pect
15	cycle	35	national
16	honest	36	noculars
17	phone	37	obey
18	atlantic	38	historic
19	wrap	39	fortune
20	stick	40	fiction

Prefixes

Prefix Splits (Answers)

Common prefixes.

Teacher's Tips

1	**non**	sense	21	**pre**	dict
2	**anti**	clockwise	22	**auto**	graph
3	**super**	market	23	**mis**	understand
4	**mis**	take	24	**re**	paint
5	**trans**	mit	25	**sub**	way
6	**inter**	rupt	26	**ex**	it
7	**sub**	marine	27	**super**	sonic
8	**tele/ super**	vision	28	**un**	lucky
9	**auto**	matic	29	**re**	lax
10	**ex/ re**	pel	30	**anti**	septic
11	**dis**	appear	31	**re**	cord
12	**inter**	net	32	**un**	willing
13	**mis/ re**	treat	33	**trans**	fer
14	**un**	kind	34	**ex**	pect
15	**bi**	cycle	35	**inter**	national
16	**dis**	honest	36	**bi**	noculars
17	**tele**	phone	37	**dis**	obey
18	**trans**	atlantic	38	**pre**	historic
19	**un**	wrap	39	**mis**	fortune
20	**non/ re**	stick	40	**non**	fiction

Families Card Game

Rules: 2–4 players

1. Photocopy onto thin card and cut out prefix squares.
2. Shuffle cards and deal six cards to each player and put the remaining cards in a pile.
3. Player 1 asks player 2 if he has a specific *prefix* family card for example an **'anti-'** family card.

   If Player 2 has an **'anti-'** card, he hands it over to Player 1 and Player 1 has another go.
4. If Player 2 doesn't have the card, Player 1 picks up from pile and the turn passes on.
5. The winner is the person who has the most families (sets of 4) at the end of game.

anti- antisocial	anti- antifreeze	anti- antibiotic
anti- antihistamine	inter- interval	inter- Internet
inter- interview	inter- interrupt	mis- mistake

Prefixes

mistreat

misunderstand

misfortune

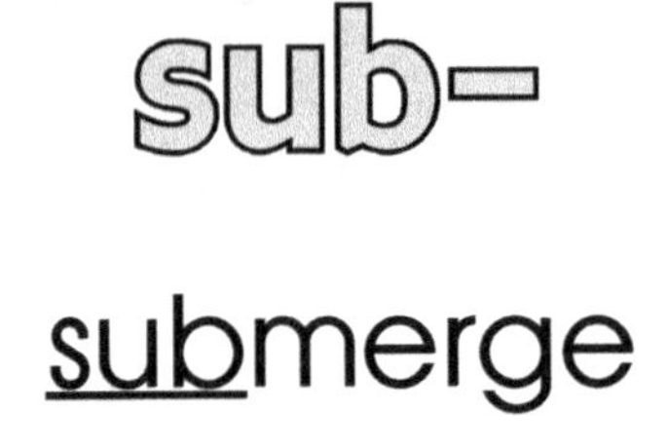

submerge

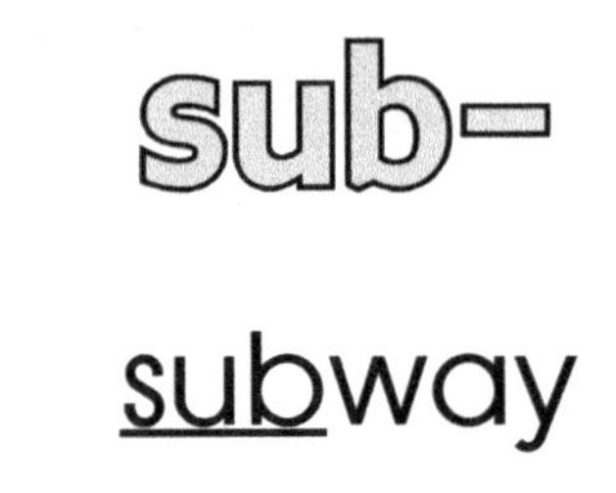

subway

sub-

subtract

sub-

submarine

transfer

trans-

transform

trans-

transatlantic

translate

auto-

autograph

auto-

autopilot

auto-

automatic

Prefixes

automobile

preview

precook

pre-

prearrange

pre-

prehistoric

super-

superman

super-

superstar

super-

supermarket

super-

supersonic

tele-

telephone

tele-

television

tele-

telegraph

tele-

telescope

dis-

disagree

misfortune

Prefixes

dis-
disappear
dis-
dishonest

dis-
disobey
re-
repeat
re-
return
re-
reaction
re-
recycle
non-
non-fiction

non-
nonsense
non-
nonstop
non-
nonprofit

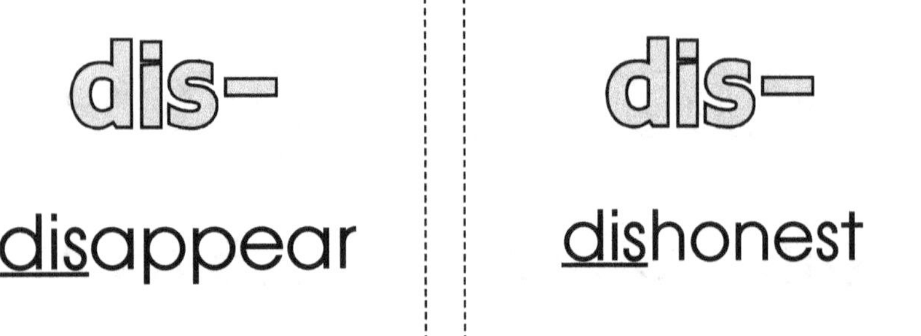

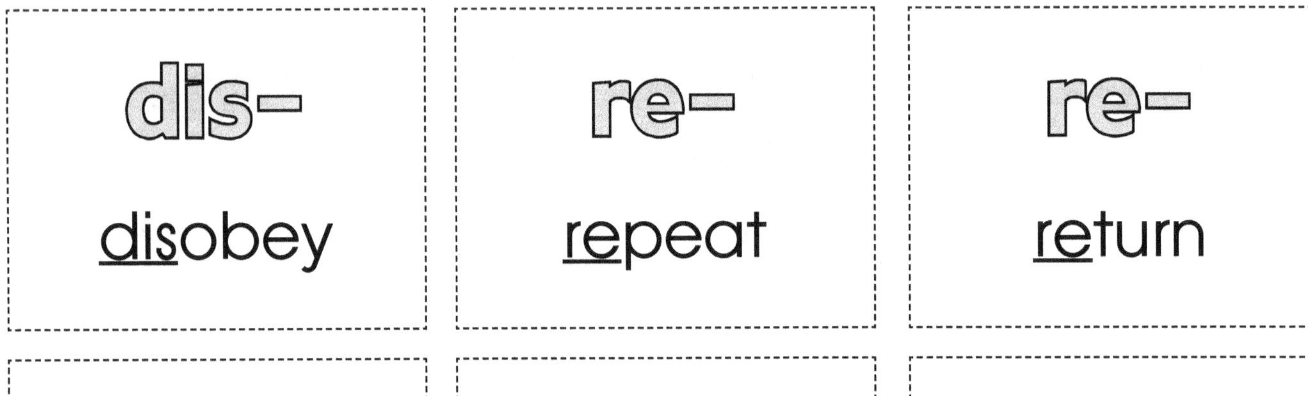

Dictation Exercises

Prefixes

NOTE: Target words are underlined.
Sentences in **bold** are harder dictation.

anti-

1. I need to have some antiseptic on that cut.
2. Dad has put some antifreeze in the car.
3. Is there an antidote for that snake's venomous bite?
4. **He always carried antihistamine for his allergy.**
5. **She had to have antibiotics to clear up the infection.**
6. **His antisocial behaviour in school got him into trouble.**

inter-

1. The world wide web is a series of pages accessible through the Internet which is a global computer network.
2. Please do not interrupt me when I am speaking.
3. In the interval, I shall get an ice cream.
4. **I hope you get an interview for that job.**
5. **Don't interfere with what he is doing.**
6. **We had a good discussion about the first scene of the play during the interlude.**

mis-

1. Do not mistreat that poor dog.
2. I think that you are mistaken about me.
3. I am sorry if I have misjudged you this time.
4. **I think that you misunderstand that question.**
5. **Their misbehaviour resulted in a punishment.**
6. **Cinderella had the misfortune to lose her glass slipper.**

Dictation Exercises

Prefixes

> **NOTE:** Target words are underlined.
> Sentences in **bold** are harder dictation.

sub-

1. Can you subtract five from ten?
2. In a second, the duck will submerge under the water.
3. The submarine could be seen above the water.
4. **I paid the annual subscription to the club yesterday.**
5. **The suburbs are always on the outskirts of the town.**
6. **The manager made a substitution in the match.**

trans-

1. I will transplant the plant into a bigger pot.
2. Can you translate the letter into English?
3. The decorator will transform your bedroom.
4. **The word transparent means you can see through it.**
5. **She had to have a blood transfusion while she was in hospital.**
6. **He has transferred some money into my bank account.**

Origins of Root Words

Modern English has developed from the root words of other languages: Greek, Latin and French in particular. At various times in the early part of our history, invaders from Europe conquered and settled in Britain. For example, the Romans spoke Latin and Greek and occupied Britain for four hundred years and later the French speaking Normans from Northern France inhabited England for nearly three centuries.

Check out words derived from **Latin** origins.

ROOT	MEANING	EXAMPLES
fort	strength	fortress, comfort, fortitude
fract /frag	break	fracture, fraction, fragile, fragment
ject	throw	eject, projector, injection
ped	foot	pedal, pedicure, pedestrian
port	carry	porter, portable, transport,
spect	watch/ examine	spectacle, spectator, inspect
struct	build	construct, instruct, destruction
tract	pull	extract, contract, retract

Check out words derived from **Greek** origins.

ROOT	MEANING	EXAMPLES
meter	measure	diameter, kilometre, speedometer
path	feeling	sympathetic, empathy, apathetic
phon	sound	telephone , microphone, phonics
scope	see	telescope, microscope, horoscope
therm	heat	thermal, thermometer, thermostat
zoon	animal/organism	zoo, zoology, protozoa, zodiac

A knowledge of the meaning of roots is useful as it can help give meaning to words that are unfamiliar!

Root Words

Origins of Root Words

A root word is a word or part of a word that can form the basis of a new word when a suffix or prefix (or both) are added.

tractor

Prefix	Root: tract	Suffix
con-	contract	-able
dis-	contractor	-ed
ex-	distract	-ible
pro-	distracted	-ing
re-	distractible	-ion
sub-	extractable	-or
	extracted	
	extraction	
	protracted	
	protractor	
	retract	
	retraction	
	subtract	
	subtracting	
	subtraction	

Root Words

How Many Can You Make?

Add the prefixes and suffixes to the root word. For example pro**ject**or. Look out for some words where you can add two prefixes or two suffixes, for example: **re-/con-/**struct**/-ing** or **ob-/**ject**/-ion/-able**.

Try doing it as a timed exercise.

PREFIXES	-struct-	-vent-	-ject-	SUFFIXES
re-				-ed
in-				-ing
ob-				-ion
de-				-or
con-				-able
sub-				-ive
ad-				-ure
pre-				
pro-				

Root Words

How Many Can You Make?

Add the prefixes and suffixes to the root word. For example pro**ject**or. Look out for some words where you can add two prefixes or two suffixes, for example: **de-/com-/**press**/-ion** or **ex-/**press**/-ive/-ly**.

Try doing it as a timed exercise.

PREFIXES	-port-	-form-	-press-	SUFFIXES
trans-				-ed
re-				-ing
ex-				-ion
con-				-able
in-				-er
ob-				-ly
com-				-ant
im-				-ive
de-				-ation

I can make ________________ words.

Possible Answers

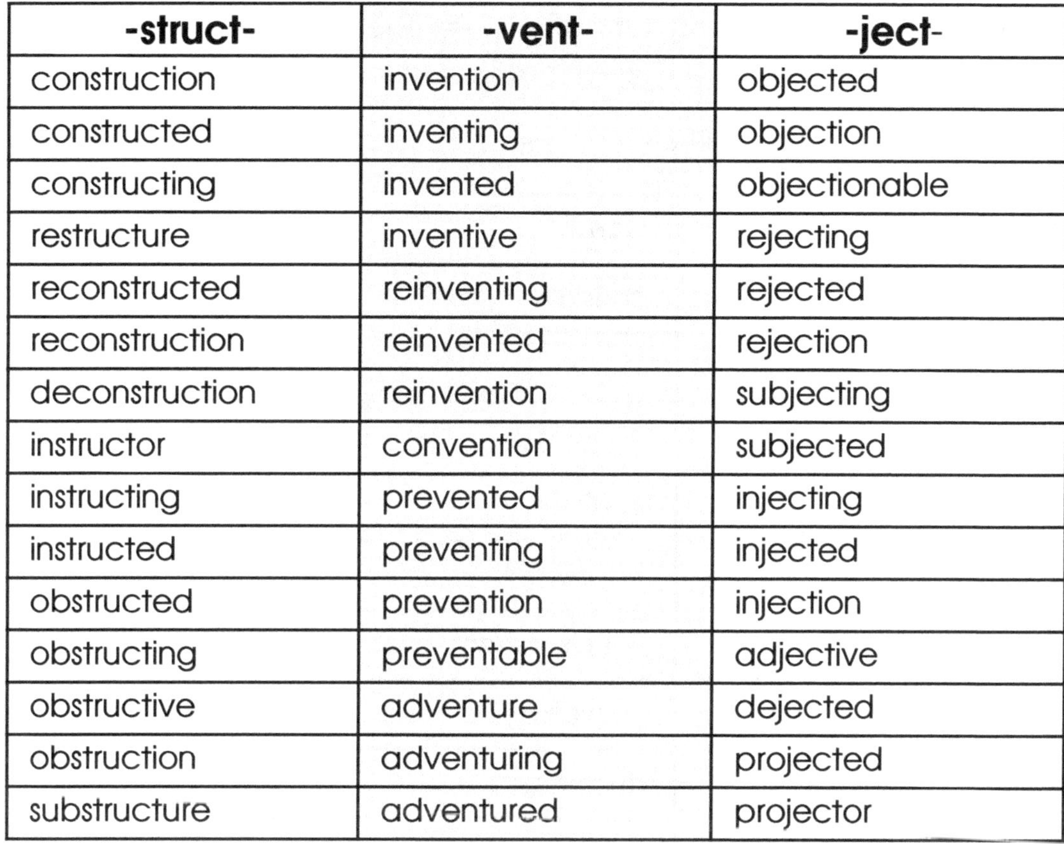

-struct-	-vent-	-ject-
construction	invention	objected
constructed	inventing	objection
constructing	invented	objectionable
restructure	inventive	rejecting
reconstructed	reinventing	rejected
reconstruction	reinvented	rejection
deconstruction	reinvention	subjecting
instructor	convention	subjected
instructing	prevented	injecting
instructed	preventing	injected
obstructed	prevention	injection
obstructing	preventable	adjective
obstructive	adventure	dejected
obstruction	adventuring	projected
substructure	adventured	projector

-form-	-port-	-press-
performing	transporting	expressing
transformed	transported	expressed
transforming	transportation	expression
transformer	transportable	expressive (ly)
transformation	exported	expressly
reformed	exporting	repressing
reforming	exporter	repressed
reformer	important	repression
informer	importantly	depression
informed	reporting	depressed
informing	reported(ly)	depressing (ly)
informant	reporter	depressive
information	deporting	impressive
conformed	deported	impressively
conforming	deportation	(de) compressed
conformation	exportation	(de) compression

Root Words

Find the Root Word

A root word is a word or part of a word that can form the basis of a new word when a suffix or prefix is added.

Write down the basic whole root word for each of the words below.

editor *edit*	signal
dislike	childish
fairest	lovely
activity	almighty
maturity	addition
discovery	heroism
indication	imprisonment
calculator	secretary
unhappiness	dishonesty
misbehaviour	reappearance

Can you add an extra word or words from the same root?

joy	joyous	enjoy		
act	actor	action		
child	childlike	childhood		
cover	uncover	recover		

Add a prefix or suffix (or both) to the words in the star to create new words.

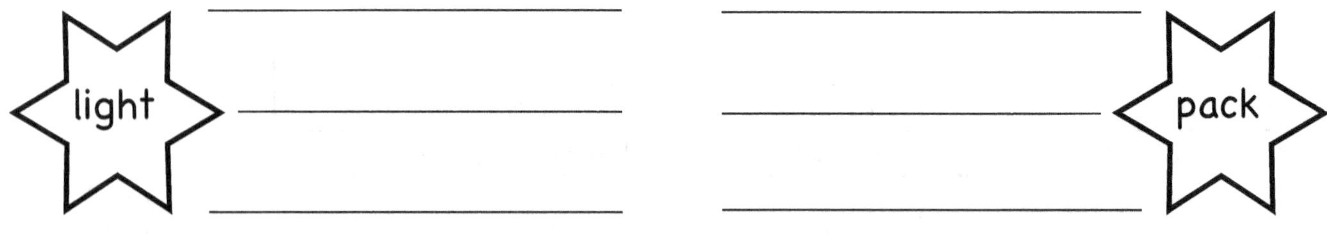

Root Words Game

A game for four players. Photocopy a full set of sheets for each player onto thin card and cut up word cards. Each pupil starts with the five shaded root word cards.

Shuffle the derivations and place face down in a pile. Pupils take it in turns to select a word card. Unwanted word cards are placed in a new pile. The first pupil to collect the full five sets of cards, their derivations and spell the words correctly wins the game.

pack	package	prepacked
joy	joyful	enjoyment
assist	assistant	assistance
cover	discover	discovery
give	given	giving

Root Words

Root Words Game

obey	disobey	disobedient
prove	approval	disapprove
call	recall	calling
light	lighting	delighted
relate	related	relation

Root Words Game

press	impress	depression
take	taken	mistaken
hero	heroic	heroism
govern	governor	government
shake	shakily	shaken

Root Words

Root Words Game

operate	cooperate	cooperation
electric	electricity	electrical
act	react	reaction
prison	imprison	imprisoned
medic	medicine	nonmedical

Suffix Spelling Rules

There are certain general guidelines for adding suffix endings to root words. Here are some common suffix rules, although be aware there are always some exceptions.

Double Letter Rule

For most **one** syllable words ending in **one** short vowel and **one** single consonant, (the 1-1-1 rule) you need to double the final consonant *to keep the vowel sound short* before adding a suffix that starts with a vowel: **'-ed'**, **'-ing'**, **'-er'**, **'-est'** or **'-y'**.

Common exceptions are base/root words ending in **'w'** and **'x'**.

For example: ***stew*: stews, stewed, stewing**
***flex*: flexes, flexing**

	Doubled letters		
	-ed	**-er**	**-ing**
rob	robbed	robber	robbing
run		runner	running
hug	hugged		hugging
win		winner	winning
clap	clapped		clapping
plan	planned	planner	planning
stop	stopped	stopper	stopping
wrap	wrapped	wrapper	wrapping

	Doubled letters				
	-ed	**-ing**	**-er**	**-est**	**-y**
sun	sunned	sunning	sunnier*	sunniest*	sunny
pop	popped	popping	popper		
run		running	runnier*	runniest*	runny
slip	slipped	slipping	slippier*	slippiest*	slippy
plan	planned	planning	planner		
spot	spotted	spotting		spottiest*	spotty

*When adding the suffixes **'-er'** and **'-est'** to words ending in a consonant plus a **'-y'**, change the **'y'** to an **'i'** before adding suffix, for example: sunny – sunnier, sunniest.

signalling

Spelling Rules

Suffix Spelling Rules

There are certain general guidelines for adding suffix endings. Check out the common suffix rules although be aware there are always some exceptions.

Teacher's Tips

Double Letter Rule

For two syllable words ending with a single vowel and a single consonant, you DOUBLE the final consonant before adding your vowel suffix if the *last syllable* is *stressed*.

For example:

be**gin**	beginner	beginning
ad**mit**	admitted	admitting
for**get**	forgetting	forgotten
pre**fer**	preferred	preferring
re**gret**	regretted	regretting
per**mit**	permitted	permitting
trans**fer**	transferred	transferring

BUT two syllable words ending in 1 vowel and 1 consonant, DO NOT double if the last syllable is not stressed.

of **fer** ing	hap **pen** ing	en **ter** ing	leng **then** ed
dif **fer** ent	gar **den** ing	pref **er** ence	ab an **don** ed

Longer words ending with a vowel and the consonant **'l'**, always DOUBLE the **'l'** before adding the vowel suffix regardless of which syllables are stressed.

For example:

signal	signalled	signalling
pedal	pedalled	pedalling
travel	travelled	traveller
enrol	enrolled	enrolling
marvel	marvelled	marvellous
cancel	cancelled	cancelling
quarrel	quarrelled	quarrelling

Note:
an exception to this rule is when you are adding a consonant suffix to the root word.
For example:
regret**ful**
enrol**ment**
quarrel**some**
commit**ment**

Spelling Rules

Suffix Spelling Rules

Double Letter Final Consonant Rule 1

For most **one** syllable words ending in **one** vowel and **one** single consonant, (the 1-1-1 rule) you need to DOUBLE the final consonant *to keep the vowel sound short* before adding a suffix that starts with a vowel: **'-ed'**, **'-ing'**, **'-er'**, **'-est'** or a **'-y'**.

Double the letter to finish these word sums.

sad + est = saddest

hid + en = ______

stop + ing = ______

pop + y = ______

wrap + er = ______

flat + er = ______

thin + est = ______

beg + ed = ______

hem + ed = ______

slip + er = ______

Double or not?

Tip: Listen for the short vowel sound and make sure it is a vowel suffix before you double.

pot + er = ______

drip + ed = ______

grin + ed = ______

sad + est = ______

fun + y = ______

big + est = ______

cup + ful = ______

sleep + ing = ______

span + ing = ______

trap + ed = ______

Choose the correct word to complete the sentence. Delete as appropriate.

1. Grandad enjoyed the roast *dinner/diner* he had on Sunday.
2. Tom was *hopping/hoping* to win first prize in the competition.
3. The postman *taped/tapped* up the parcel as it was undone.
4. She was *filling/filing* up the watering can in the garden.
5. Ruby *hopped/hoped* she would get a bike for her birthday.
6. Mum *scrapped/scraped* the cake mixture from off the bowl.
7. "Please put the *coma/comma* in the sentence," said the teacher.
8. She *pinned/pined* the pictures on the wall in the kitchen.
9. The zebra had *striped/stripped* markings on its back.
10. He had *planned/planed* to go to Spain for a holiday.

Spelling Rules

Suffix Spelling Rules

Double Letter Final Consonant Rule 2

For two syllable words ending in one vowel and one consonant, DOUBLE the final consonant *to keep vowel short* before adding vowel suffix when last syllable is stressed.

forge**t**	forge**tt**ing	forgo**tt**en	forge**tt**able

Add the correct suffix **'-ed'** or **'-ing'** to modify the words in brackets.

Tip: Don't forget to double!

1. We all ______________________ from having had the extra coaching. (benefit)
2. The man ______________________ at last that he had stolen the jewellery. (admit)
3. I keep ______________________ to close my wardrobe door. (forget)
4. He ______________________ to have an icecream rather than a cake. (prefer)
5. Tom ______________________ in his exams – he got top marks! (excel)
6. Are you ______________________ us to go to the festival next week? (permit)
7. My brother is ______________________ in the scouts this evening. (enrol)
8. It was ______________________ to hear that we couldn't go on holiday. (upset)
9. Nick was ______________________ from school because of his bad behaviour. (expel)
10. The girl was ______________________ because her leg was in plaster. (handicap)
11. Jack really ______________________ he had not revised for the exam. (regret)
12. At last Poppy is ______________________ to feel a lot better. (begin)
13. I hope you are ______________________ from all your hard work. (profit)
14. "Are you ______________________ with the right tools for the job?" (equip)

Spelling Rules

Suffix Spelling Rules

Double Letter Final Consonant Rule 2

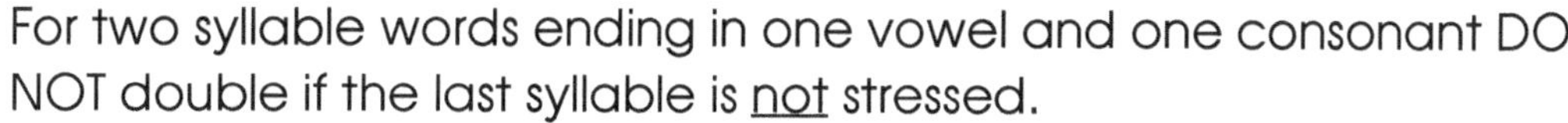

For two syllable words ending in one vowel and one consonant DO NOT double if the last syllable is not stressed.

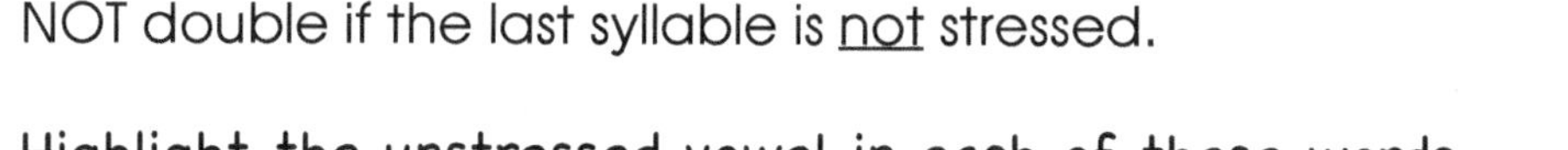

Highlight the unstressed vowel in each of these words.

Tip: Say the word out loud to hear if the second syllable is emphasised.

fastened	gardener	suffering
wondering	preference	frightening
camera	generous	library

Choose a word from the box above to complete the sentence.

1. He had ____________________ his shoe laces so they would not come undone.
2. The ____________________ mowed the grass and weeded the flower beds.
3. Molly had a ____________________ for chips rather than mashed potato.
4. I was ____________________ would be all right if Sara came for tea later?
5. My brother was ____________________ from heat stroke and felt very poorly.
6. All the talk about ghosts was ____________________ the young child.
7. Please can you tale all these books back to the ____________________ .
8. She was very ____________________ to give me so much money.
9. He took a lovely photograph of the sunset with his new ____________________ .

Spelling Rules ______________

Suffix Spelling Rules

Double Letter Rule 3

For words with two syllables that end with one vowel and one consonant where the last syllable is stressed, you DOUBLE the final consonant before adding the vowel suffix ie, regre**t** = *regretted* or kidna**p** = *kidnapped*.

For multi-syllable words that end with a vowel and an **'l'**, you ALWAYS DOUBLE the **'l'** even if the last syllable is not stressed, for example: trave**l** = *traveller*, signal = *signalling*.

If adding a consonant suffix such as **'-ful'**, **'-ly'** or **'-ment'** to words ending in one vowel and one consonant, DO NOT DOUBLE.

Stressed or not?

control + ing ______________ refer + ed ______________

interest + ed ______________ occur + ence ______________

kidnap + er ______________ pedal + ing ______________

lengthen + ed ______________ equip + ment ______________

infer + ence ______________ regret + ing ______________

Double or not?

Write the word correctly to complete the sentence.

1. The (*propel + er*) **propeller** of the plane was damaged in the storm.
2. The meaning of (*lengthen + ing*) ______________ is to make longer.
3. Have you (*transfer + ed*) ______________ the money to my bank today?
4. I have always (*regret + ed*) ______________ not saying goodbye.
5. Are you (*listen + ing*) ______________to anything that I am saying?
6. Using hosepipes is (*forbid + en*) ______________ in a drought situation.
7. Are you (*travel + ing*) ______________ to London on the coach?
8. Gran is very (*forget + ful*) ______________ so she often mislays her glasses.
9. He was put in the (*begin + er*) ______________s class as he could not swim.
10. I can see many people (*marvel + ing*) ______________ at the huge moon.

Suffix Spelling Rules: 'e' Rule

There are certain general guidelines for adding suffix endings. Check out the common suffix rules although be aware there are always some exceptions.

DROP the **'e'** before adding a vowel suffix: **'-ing'**, **'-ed'**, **'-er'**, **'-able'**, or **'-y'**.

For example:

	-ed	-ing	-er	-able	-y
achieve	achieved	achieving	achiever	achievable	
admire	admired	admiring	admirer	admirable	admirably
believe	believed	believing	believer	believable	believably
desire	desired	desiring	desirer	desirable	desirably
divide	divided	dividing	divider	dividable	
love	loved	loving	lover	lovable	
move	moved	moving	mover	movable	
taste	tasteable	tasted	taster	tasting	tasty

KEEP the **'e'** before adding a consonant suffix: **'-ful'**, **'-less'**, **'-ly'**, **'-ment'**.

	-ful	-less	-ly	-ment
base		baseless		basement
care	careful	careless	carelessly	
home		homeless	homely	
love		loveless	lovely	
state		stateless	stately	statement
use	useful	useless		

KEEP the **'e'** if words end in **'ce'** or **'ge'** before adding **'-able'** (to keep **'c'** or **'g'** soft).

change	changeable	notice	noticeable
charge	manageable	replace	replaceable
knowledge	knowledgeable	service	serviceable
manage	manageable	trace	traceable

Spelling Rules ______________

Suffix Spelling Rules

'e' Rule

DROP the **'e'** before adding the vowel suffix: **'-ing'**, **'-ed'**, **'-er'**, **'-ous'**, **'-able'** or **'-y'**. Only **KEEP** the **'e'** if adding **'-able'** to words ending in **'ce'** or **'ge'** to keep 'c' or 'g' soft, ie changeable.

Can you complete these words correctly?

close + ed = ______________ decide + ing = ______________

write + er = ______________ grease + y = ______________

dance + ing = ______________ fame + ous = ______________

taste + ing = ______________ value + able = ______________

KEEP the **'e'** if you are adding a consonant suffix: **'-ful'**, **'-less'**, **'-ly'** and **'-ment'**, and also when adding **'-able'** to words ending in **'-ce'** or **'-ge'** to keep c/g soft'.

grace + ful = ______________ use + less = ______________

love + ly = ______________ notice + able = ______________

amaze + ment = ______________ hope + ful = ______________

rude + ness = ______________ manage + able = ______________

Write the word in brackets correctly to complete the following sentences. Add a vowel suffix **'-able'**, **'-ed'** or **'-ing'**. Think whether you need to keep or drop the 'e'.

1. Mum was busy ______________ a birthday cake. (bake)
2. The door ______________ in the wind with a bang. (close)
3. "This diamond ring is very ______________". (value)
4. He is ______________ up to buy a new car. (save)
5. The weather will be ______________ with rain and sunny spells. (change)

Write the word correctly in the bracket to complete the sentences.
Add a consonant suffix: **'-ful'**, **'-less'**, **'-ly'** or **'-ment'** Do you keep or drop the 'e'?

1. The watch was ______________ because it did not work. (use)
2. Much to her ______________ she had won the lottery! (amaze)
3. Be ______________ not to lose the concert tickets. (care)
4. She is ______________ going to the birthday party. (definite)

Suffix Spelling Rules: 'y' rule

There are certain general guidelines for adding suffix endings. Check out the common suffix rules although be aware there are some exceptions.

For words ending in consonant plus **'y'**, CHANGE **'y'** to **'i'** and add the suffix. Examples:

easy	easier	easiest	easily
busy	busier	busiest	busily
lazy	lazier	laziest	lazily
pretty	prettier	prettiest	prettily
heavy	heavier	heaviest	heavily
rely	relies	relied	reliable
vary	varies	varied	variable
worry	worries	worried	worrisome
justify	justifies	justified	justifiable
supply	supplies	supplied	supplier
happy	happier	happiness	happily

For words ending in vowel plus **'y'**, – KEEP **'y'** and add suffix. For example:

play	player	playful	playing
enjoy	enjoyed	enjoyment	enjoying
spray	sprayed	sprayer	spraying
annoy	annoys	annoyed	annoying
survey	surveys	surveyor	surveying

When adding **'-ing'** to words ending in **'y'**, KEEP **'y'** and add suffix. For example:

hurrying	copying	supplying	delaying
carrying	magnifying	occupying	straying

Teacher's Tips

Spelling Rules

Suffix Spelling Rules: 'y' rule

When a word ends with 'y', change the 'y' to an 'i' and add a suffix. (Remember: Keep the 'y' if adding '-ing'.)

cry + ed = cried

easy + er = ____________

rely + able = ____________

hurry + ing = ____________

spy + ed = ____________

heavy + est = ____________

supply + er = ____________

reply + ed = ____________

Keep the 'y'

(Remember: Keep the 'y' if there is a vowel before the 'y' or if adding '-ing'.)

delay + ed = ____________

play + ful = ____________

donkey + s = ____________

annoy + ance = ____________

enjoy + ment = ____________

spray + er = ____________

apply + ing = ____________

survey + ed = ____________

Change or keep the 'y'?

hurry + ed = ____________

clumsy + ly = ____________

beauty + ful = ____________

destroy + er = ____________

annoy + ed = ____________

carry + ing = ____________

lazy + ness = ____________

multiply + ed = ____________

Add a correct suffix to the word in brackets to complete the sentence. (Remember to check if you have to change or keep the 'y'.)

1. The farmer ____________ eggs to the village shop. (supply)
2. The art work was ____________ on the classroom wall. (display)
3. Tom ____________ down the road to catch the bus. (hurry)
4. The little girl was ____________ as she had fallen off her bike. (cry)
5. The red roses looked very ____________ in the garden. (beauty)
6. He was ____________ on an aeroplane to America tonight. (fly)
7. "Two ____________ by six equals twelve," said Poppy. (multiply)
8. He was ____________ going to play football every Saturday. (enjoy)

signalling

Suffix Spelling Rules: '-ful' rule

There are certain general guidelines for adding suffix endings. Check out the common suffix rules although be aware there are some exceptions.

'-ful' rule

Rule: The suffix '-**ful**' means '*full of*' but the '**ll**' becomes '**l**' when used as a suffix. It is used to change a noun into an adjective.

For example:

hope	hopeful	boast	boastful	fright	frightful
hurt	hurtful	doubt	doubtful	wonder	wonderful
care	careful	truth	truthful	faith	faithful
pain	painful	power	powerful	thank	thankful
fear	fearful	thought	thoughtful	colour	colourful
peace	peaceful	fate	fateful	success	successful
faith	faithful	colour	colourful	wonder	wonderful

When words end in a consonant plus y change '**y**' to '**i**' when adding '-**ful**'.

For example:

pity	pitiful	mercy	merciful	fancy	fanciful
duty	dutiful	beauty	beautiful	plenty	plentiful

When changing words ending '-**ful**', eg, *joyful*, to an adverb, the suffix will change to 'll', ie, *joyfully*.
For example:

joyful	joyfully	cheerful	cheerfully	spiteful	spitefully
playful	playfully	wasteful	wastefully	graceful	gracefully
grateful	gratefully	regretful	regretfully	fearful	fearfully
helpful	helpfully	careful	carefully	hopeful	hopefully

Spelling Rules

Suffix Spelling Rules: '-ful' rule

Rule: The suffix **'-ful'** means *'full of'* but the **'ll'** becomes **'l'** when used as a suffix. It is used to change a noun into an adjective.

Complete the word sums. Remember if the word ends in **'y'** change to an **'i'** before you add the suffix.

cheer + ful = ______________________ hope + ful = ______________________

plenty + ful = ______________________ thank + ful = ______________________

wonder + ful = ______________________ beauty + ful = ______________________

mercy + ful = ______________________ forget + ful = ______________________

Change the suffix from **'-less'** to **'-ful'** to give the opposite meaning.

careless = ______________________ harmless = ______________________

fearless = ______________________ hopeless = ______________________

helpless = ______________________ restless = ______________________

meaningless = ______________________ doubtless = ______________________

Add **'-ly'** to change **'-ful'** word into an adverb. Then write a sentence using the new word.

Tip: When a word ending **'-ful'** is changed into an adverb, the suffix will have **'ll'** for example: playful – playfully
Playfully, the kitten chased the clockwork mouse round the room.

1. helpful = ______________________

____

2. cheerful = ______________________

____

3. hopeful = ______________________

____

4. careful = ______________________

____

5. wonderful = ______________________

____

Suffix Spelling Rules: '-ful' rule

Rule: The suffix '-**ful**' means '*full of*' but the '**ll**' becomes '**l**' when used as a suffix. It is used to change a noun into an adjective.

doubtful	painful	spiteful	fearful	powerful
tearful	plentiful	joyful	beautiful	meaningful

Choose a word from the box above that has the same meaning as one below.

very pretty	=	unsure	=
frightened	=	happy	=
nasty	=	lots of	=
sore and tender	=	strong	=
upset	=	having purpose	=

Use the words you have chosen to fill in the missing gaps below.

1. I am ______________________ that our house is going to flood.
2. It is ______________________ whether I can play football.
3. The red roses in the garden look very ______________________.
4. My ankle is very ______________________ since I fell off the swing.
5. The tall trees swayed in the ______________________ wind.
6 The boy was ______________________ when he called me names.
7 He was ______________________ that he had come first in the race.
8. The sad news made the woman feel ______________________ .
9. There is a ______________________ amount of money in the bank.
10. The tests did not produce any ______________________ results.

Can you find the root word?

unhelpful		pitiful	
beautiful		wonderfully	
ungracefully		insightful	
plentifully		unmerciful	

Spelling Rules

'ie' or 'ei' Rule?

Can you spell these words?

ei		ie	
beige	receipt	relief	ancient
eighty	foreign	niece	grieving
weight	caffeine	briefly	efficient
sleigh	protein	shriek	achievement
seized	deceiving	mischief	handkerchief
receive	neighbour	interview	achievable
perceive	reindeer	oriental	hygienic
deceitful	misconceive	besieged	conscience
conceited	inconceivable	science	unbelievable
ceiling	transceiver	diesel	inconvenience

Guidance:

'ie' Many words use **ie** to make a long **/e/** vowel sound.

'ei' Used to make a long **/e/** vowel sound if **c** is before **ie**
or when you can hear a long **/a/** vowel sound

(Useful mnemonic "**i** before **e** except after **C**" or when sounded as a long **'a'** sound)

Common exceptions: ancient, seize, conscience, view, science, caffeine, protein.

Write sentences using some of the words from the box above.

1. ______________________________

2. ______________________________

3. ______________________________

4. ______________________________

5. ______________________________

Spelling Rules

'ie' or 'ei' Words

Read the passage and highlight the **'ie'** and **'ei'** words.

All at once I heard Molly Priest, my next door neighbour give a loud shriek. For a brief moment I thought something awful had happened. As Molly had been unwell and only recently come out of hospital, I rushed over to see her and it was a relief to discover everything was alright. However, something inconceivable had happened. Molly had just been notified that she'd inherited eight million pounds from a distant rich relative! I was delighted that she had received such a piece of good fortune as things had been tough for her lately. Molly could not quite believe her luck but the following day she was besieged by the local press who had discovered her news. Molly had some initial ideas about how she would spend the money. First of all she intended to take her family for a fabulous holiday to the Seychelles, in the middle of the Indian Ocean, as she'd never had a holiday. It would also give her great pleasure to buy her niece Lucy, who had recently married, a little flat in town. Lucy had been worth her weight in gold during her aunt's prolonged stay in hospital visiting her regularly and looking after her dog. She would buy her grandson the most fiendish go-cart it was possible to buy. In fact, Molly perceived countless ways, as you can imagine, on how she could spend her newly acquired wealth.

Can you split these words up into syllables?

u n b e l i e v e a b l e
d e c e i t f u l n e s s
i n d e s t r u c t i b l e
u n d e r a c h i e v e m e n t

Spelling Rules

'ie' or 'ei' Words

When you hear a long '**e**' vowel sound use '**ie**' but use '**ei**' after **c** or when you can hear the long **a** vowel sound.
Complete the words by putting in '**ie**' or '**ei**' in the spaces.

bel ve	c ling	prot n
p ce	shr k	ach ve
for gn	s zed	misch f
d sel	perc ve	n ghbour

Choose the correct word from the words below to complete the sentences.

relieved	besieged	caffeine	hygienically	received
reindeer	deceitful	eighty	handkerchief	receipt

1. The number seventy nine comes before ________________ .
2. The pop star was ________________ by photographers.
3. The kitchen was ________________ clean for cooking purposes.
4. It is ________________ not to tell the truth about things.
5. Please blow your nose with that paper ________________ .
6. Did Rudolph the ________________ help pull Santa's sleigh?
7. I felt ________________ that I did not have my tooth extracted.
8. Keep the till ________________ if you want to take the shirt back.
9. ________________ is found in many drinks such as coffee and tea.
10. Yesterday I ________________ a letter in the post from my Granny.

Match the word with its meaning.

Word	Meaning
besiege	Belonging to the very distant past
conceited	Dishonest, hiding the truth
hygienic	Unbelievable, impossible to imagine
deceitful	To overrun or crowd around
ancient	Too proud of yourself, vain
inconceivable	Clean in order to prevent disease

Dictation Exercises

To Spell Target Words Correctly

NOTE: Target words are underlined.

Double letter rule

1. I think July was the hottest month of the year.
2. He stopped to get a poppy for his mum.
3. Gran was *busy* knitting me a red jumper.
4. She hummed a little tune while washing up.
5. "What are you grinning at?" said Nigel.
6. Milly took up jogging to *develop* her fitness.
7. My friend wrapped the gift in silver paper.
8. I had forgotten to bring my *favourite* hat with me.
9. We all benefitted from eating lots of *fruit* and *vegetables.*
10. You are not permitted to walk on the grass!

'e' rule

1. The nurse was a caring person.
2. The boy made a lot of careless mistakes.
3. I was hoping to see my friend on Wednesday.
4. Tom was hopeful that he could play in the match.
5. Mum was liking the coat she got in the sale.
6. It is very likely that it will rain today.
7. "I am not changing my mind," said Jill.
8. Can the weather be very changeable in *February?*
9. It is exciting we are all going away on holiday.
10. There was excitement when the popstar left the *yacht.*

'y' rule

1. Jack is hurrying down the road to catch the bus.
2. My sister hurries to finish her homework.
3. We are flying to America this Sunday.
4. There are a lot of flies by the canal today.
5. Megan is a tidier person than her sister.
6. I am very busy tidying up the messy room.
7. The clothes dried quickly outside on the line.
8. Dad is carrying all of our cases to the car.
9. The carrier bag is full up with bags of *potatoes.*
10. She felt happier that the donkeys were better looked after.

Dictation Exercises

NOTE: Target words are underlined.

'ful' rule

1. Plastics are very harmful to the environment if thrown away.
2. It's very doubtful that it will snow tomorrow as it's too warm.
3. Ahmed was very careful when he cut the pototoes into chips.
4. Cheerfully, Miss Andrews stood on stage and accepted her award.
5. The old classroom had been wonderfully redecorated with vibrant colours and lots of new posters.
6. The old lady walked over to us with an air of gracefulness.

'ei' rule

1. He tried to lift the box, but its weight was far too heavy.
2. The church ceiling was very high and had a lovely fresco painted on it.
3. I kept the till receipt, so I could exchange the trousers if they didn't fit.
4. My parents had decided that we would have a foreign holiday this year.
5. Incredulously, I was one of the eight people picked for the team.
6. The army has now seized control of the city.

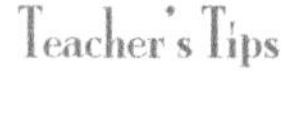

'ie' rule

1. Both petrol and diesel cars are being phased out in favour of electric ones.
2. In the brief moment as I turned my head, I swear I saw a ghost!
3. My aunty, uncle and niece came to visit us when they flew over from Italy.
4. The ancient Pyramids of Giza are thought to date back over 4,500 years .
5. My little dog is so full of mischief, he's always chewing something.
6. Before you eat your dinner, it's hygienic to wash your hands.

sail/sale

Homophones

Homophones are words that sound the same but have different meanings. They also mainly have different spellings. The word homophone originates from the Greek words *homo* (same) and *phon* (sound).

ascent	the act of climbing up	**assent**	to agree to
aloud	out loud	**allowed**	something that is permitted
cereal	breakfast food	**serial**	a story in parts
desert	a large dry barren region	**dessert**	sweet course of a meal
draft	first attempt at writing	**draught**	a current of air
father	a male parent	**farther**	at or by a great distance
guessed	predicted something	**guest**	a visitor
morning	time before lunch	**mourning**	sadness at someone's death
muscle	part of the body	**mussel**	edible sea being
passed	was successful in an exam	**past**	a previous time
practise*	(verb) to rehearse or to prepare for something	**practice***	(noun) the act of doing something daily/ a rehearsal
profit	money made in selling things	**prophet**	a person who can foretell the future
stationery	writing material (paper and envelopes)	**stationary**	not moving, still

* **Example:**

Whilst warming up for the opera, it is common practi**ce** to practi**se** your vocal scales.

The doctor had practi**s**ed medicine at his practi**c**e for over ten years.

sail/sale

Homophones

Homophones

Homophones are words that sound the same but have different meanings. They also have different spellings. The word *homophone* originates from the Greek words *homo* (same) and *phon* (sound).

Underline the correct word.

1. He was delighted to have past/passed all of his exams.
2. The woman was fined/find for parking her car without a ticket.
3. The robber was going to steel/steal the gold necklace.
4. The boy was mourning/morning the loss of his uncle.
5. Tom was pleased it was treacle toffee pudding for desert/dessert.
6. The principal/principle source of energy on Earth is the Sun.
7. I saw the strong man flex his muscles/mussels and lift the weights.
8. We were not aloud/allowed to stay up after nine o'clock.

Write the correct homophone in the space.

1. *heard or herd*

   The ____________________ of cattle are in the top field on the farm.

   I have just ____________________ the news about the plane crash!

2. *Who's or whose*

   ____________________ turn is it to do the weekly shop?

   ____________________ the girl that has lost her homework?

3. *father or farther*

   My mother and ____________________ both like to go swimming.

   My cousin asked me if we had much ____________________ to walk.

4. *plane or plain*

   The ____________________ flew across the Atlantic Ocean to New York.

   I need some ____________________ paper to print out my work.

5. grate or great

   There is a ____________________ film on television tonight.

   Mum said to ____________________ the cheese before using it.

Homophones

sail/sale

Near Homophones

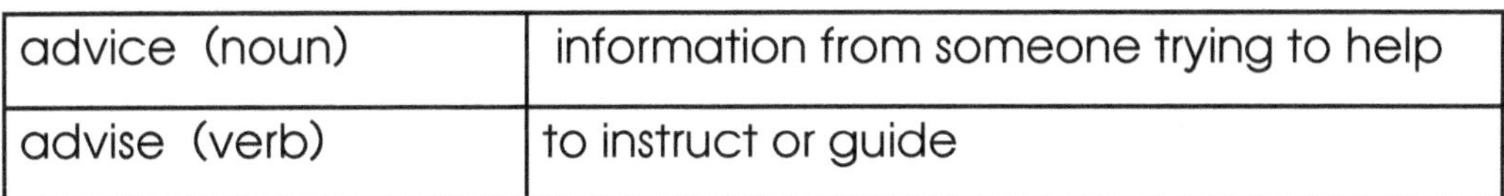

advice (noun)	information from someone trying to help
advise (verb)	to instruct or guide

practice (noun)	preparation /rehearsal
practise (verb)	to prepare /to rehearse

device (noun)	a tool designed for a particular task
devise (verb)	to think of an idea

conscience (noun)	a sense of right or wrong
conscious (verb)	to be awake or aware of something

Circle the correct word spelling.

1. We need to device/devise a plan to help the old lady.
2. What is the device/devise called that knocks nails into the wall?
3. It is important to practice/practise your part in the play.
4. Tonight we will have the final practise/practice for the play.
5. "Thank you for that good advise/advice" said Jack.
6. The teacher will advice/advise you on the new homework.
7. After seeing two boys bullying another, Jack's conscious/conscience got the better of him.
8. It was her first stage performance and Jill was conscious/conscience of the audience watching her.

sail/sale

Homophones

Homophone Game 1

1. Photocopy and stick the boards onto light card.
2. Cut up words on board 2 into individual squares.
3. Mix up the word squares and lay them on the table so you can see them clearly.
4. Roll the die and select a corresponding number from board 1. Answer the clue from the words in front of you.
5. Take it in turns to throw the die and pick a word to match it with the written homophone clue.
6. The winner is the first person to complete the whole board.

Board 1

Steps to another level 4	A pudding after main course 5	A dry barren landscape 6	Chewed and swallowed food 1
A long fixed look 3			A number 2
A hollow place in the ground 2			To change appearance or shape 3
The entire object 1	A delicious fruit 6	A set consisting of two items 5	Table at the front of a church 4

Homophone Game 1

Board 2

hole	dessert	stare
desert	whole	pair
pear	eight	stair
ate	alter	altar

Answers: Starting from bottom left hand corner on Board 1, going up and around:
1. whole 2. hole 3. stare 4.stair 5. desert. 6. dessert 1. ate 2. eight 3. alter 4. altar 5. pair 6. pear

sail/sale

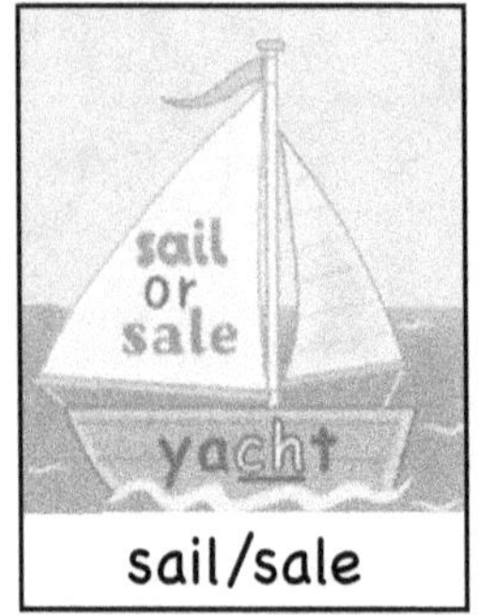

Homophones

Homophone Game 2

Board 1

Crying uncontrollably 4	A part of something 5	A person who foretells of future events 6	An island 1
The space between rows of seats 3	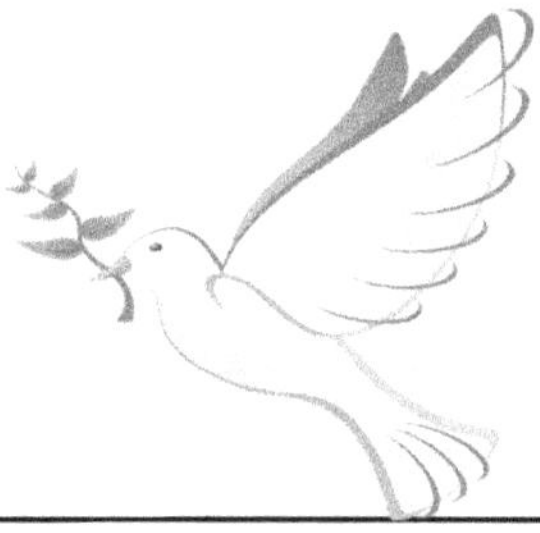	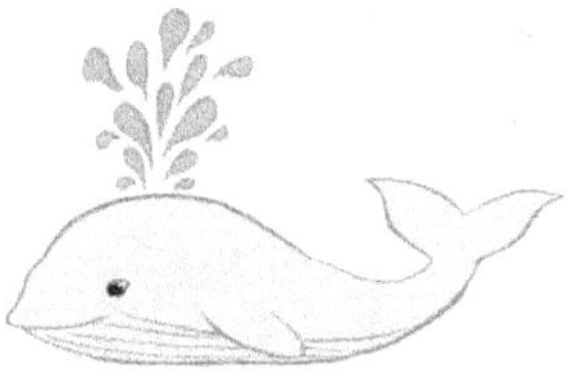	Large sea mammal 2
Money made from selling things 2	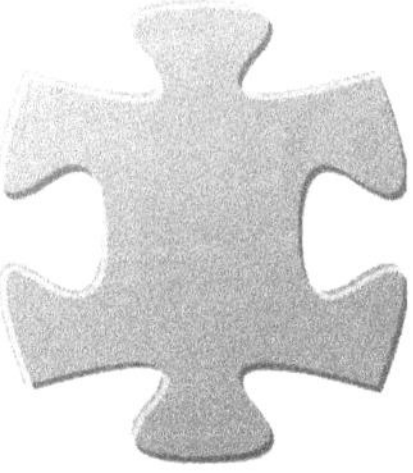	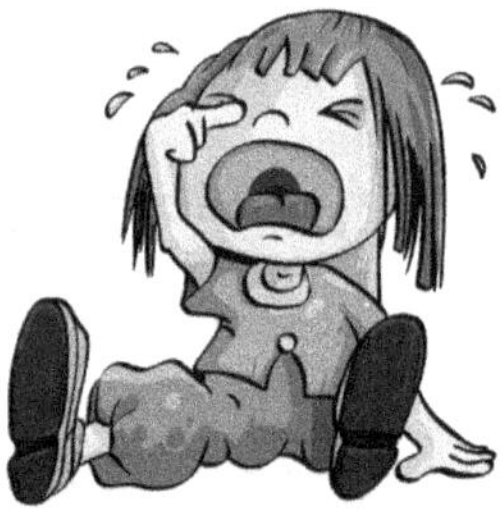	Place underground 3
A juicy fruit full of goodness 1	Belonging to us 6	Calm, serenity 5	Unit of time 4

sail or sale yacht

sail/sale

Homophone Game 2

Board 2

isle	peace	hour
berry	aisle	profit
bury	wail	piece
whale	our	prophet

Answers: Starting from bottom left hand corner on Board 1, going up and around:

1. berry 2. profit 3. aisle 4. wail 5. piece 6. prophet 1. isle 2. whale 3. bury 4. hour 5. peace 6. our

Dictation Exercises

Homophones

past/passed

We drove past the church on the way to town.
Sam passed the ball to Tom in the football game.

guest/guessed

I'm going to be staying at Blakely Hall as a guest of her ladyship.
Look at the clue. Have you guessed what it is yet?

muscle/mussel

The 'Body Builder' competitor began his show by flexing all his muscles.
I saw some empty mussel shells on the beach.

allowed/aloud

Please can you read your poem aloud to me.
You are not allowed to talk when doing the test.

desert/dessert

Are you having some apple crumble for dessert?
Don't desert me because I will be all alone.

father/farther

My father often has to go abroad on business trips.
The walk to the station was much farther than she realised.

profit/prophet

It is far better to make a profit than a loss.
People flocked from far and wide to hear the prophet speak.

morning/mourning

The birds were singing happily in the trees this morning.
The older girl was mourning the recent loss of her mother.

heard/herd

I heard the sound of a thunderclap in the sky.
The sheepdog led the herd of sheep into the pens.

cereal/serial

What cereal do you like to eat for breakfast?
She is watching the latest cartoon serial of Mr Bean.

gnome

Silent Letters

Silent letters are letters that cannot be heard when the word is pronounced. More than half of the letters in the English language alphabet are silent in some words.

Here are a few!

Silent b	Silent c	Silent g	Silent d	Silent n
lamb	scent	sign	hedge	hymn
comb	descend	gnome	bridge	autumn
numb	crescent	reign	sandwich	column
climb	science	length	handsome	condemn
thumb	muscle	design	Wednesday	solemn
debt	scenery	resign		
doubt	scissors	foreign		
plumber	fascinate	sovereign		

Silent k	Silent h	Silent t	Silent w	Silent u
knee	echo	often	wrap	guess
knot	hour	castle	write	guest
knew	when	listen	wrist	guide
knead	wheel	fasten	wrong	guard
kneel	honest	glisten	whose	build
knife	school	thistle	whole	disguise
knight	while	whistle	sword	guitar
knock	whether	ballet	answer	biscuit
knuckle	stomach	moisten	wriggle	guilty
knowledge	mechanic	Christmas	wrinkle	tongue

NB: Check out silent letters in these keywords: i**s**land; ras**p**berry; cu**p**board

gnome

Silent Letters

Silent Letters

Choose a word from the box to complete the sentences.

scent	sandwich	lamb	whistle	foreign	ghost
knowledge	handsome	scissors	plumber	answer	cupboard

1. I have just had a cheese and ham ________________ for lunch.
2. The sharp ________________ cut the thick string easily.
3. The ________________ of the perfumed roses wafted into the air.
4. Did you really think that old house was haunted by a ________________ .
5. The referee blew his ________________ to stop the football game.
6. The tiny ________________ huddled close to the mother sheep.
7. The doctor had a lot of ________________ about tropical medicines.
8. "I really don't know the ________________ to the question," said Mark.
9. The ________________ student could hardly speak any English.
10. "I have put all the shopping away in the ________________ " said Dad.
11. Do we need a ________________ to install the washing machine?
12. The ________________ prince danced with Cinderella at the ball.

Circle the silent letters.

g u e s s	r e s i g n	d o u b t
a u t u m n	g l i s t e n	m u s c l e
b i s c u i t	w h e t h e r	h o n e s t
g n o m e	s c i e n t i s t	d e s i g n

YES or **NO?** Read the following questions and circle the answer.

Is rhubarb a vegetable?	YES	NO
Is an ascent an upward climb?	YES	NO
Does Wednesday come before Friday?	YES	NO
Can you see leaves falling from trees in autumn?	YES	NO

gnome

Silent Letters

Make up a story. Look at the **'silent h'** words in the table below.

How many can you weave into your short story?

Silent h words					
chaos	chaotic	school	mechanic	vehicle	exhaust
while	choir	echoed	hour	whistling	when
orchids	whether	spaghetti	gherkin	rhubarb	what
why	honestly	exhausted	ghastly	headache	neighbour

Sentence starter ideas:

Recently	All at once	Then	After that	Furthermore	Meanwhile
Nevertheless	Even though	However	Eventually		

Dictation Exercises

Silent Letters

NOTE: Target words are underlined.
Sentences in **bold** are harder dictation.

Silent c

1. I smelled the scent of the flowers in the garden.
2. Where does the opening scene of the play take place?
3. Please do not cut yourself with those sharp scissors.
4. **The scientist was fascinated by our unusual experiment.**
5. **The abscess on my tooth was hurting in the science lesson.**

Silent g

1. Did a little mouse gnaw through that bit of wood?
2. I think I have been bitten on my elbow by a gnat.
3. The writing on that old signpost was not very clear.
4. **The foreign student was extremely happy to stay with me.**
5. **The design was based on a different length of garden.**

Silent h

1. She was teaching her little brother a rhyme.
2. To be honest I have not got any free time this week.
3. They say that a young girl's ghost haunts the house.
4. **The school cook was busy today making twenty rhubarb pies.**
5. **The mechanic can replace the broken exhaust pipe next Tuesday.**

Silent n

1. We all stood up in the hall to sing the hymn.
2. The leaves start to fall off the trees in autumn.
3. Can you add up the numbers in this column first?
4. **The judge will condemn the man to a long sentence for the crime.**
5. **The teacher gave us the sad news with a solemn expression.**

Silent u

1. How long will it take them to build the new house?
2. There are twenty guests staying in the hotel tonight.
3. We would have been lost without the guide book.
4. **Can you guess how many chocolate biscuits are in that tin?**
5. **There is no guarantee that my uncle will be found not guilty.**

Appendix 1
GLOSSARY

Analogy

Spelling by *analogy* is using the sound pattern of one word to make a prediction about the spelling pattern of a similar sounding word. In other words, using known words to spell unfamiliar ones.

For example: **could, should, would**.

Base word and Root word

A *base word* is the stand alone basic word that can also form other words when a prefix or a suffix is added.

For example: **'pack'** is the base word of: packet, package, unpack, repacked, etc.

A *root word* is a word or part of a word that can form a meaningful word when a prefix or suffix is added. It has its origins in an old Greek or Latin word.

For example: **'struct'** coming from the latin 'to build' is the root word of construct, destruct, instruct, destruction, etc.

Compound words

Compound words are made when two words are joined together to form a new word. The two words make sense on their own and the new word makes sense as well.

For example: 'toothpaste' and 'heavyweight'.

Homophones

Homophones are two or more words that sound the same but have different meanings and usually have different spellings.

For example: rain (liquid water), reign (rule as a monarch) and rein (horse lead).

Mnemonic

A *mnemonic* uses a pattern of letters, ideas, or associations to help jog the memory into remembering a difficult word to spell.

For example: There is '*a rat*' in separate.

Multisensory approach

This is the simultaneous use of visual, auditory and kinesthetic-tactile prompts which research shows enhances memory and learning.

For example: Use of '*Look, Say, Cover, Write Check*' spelling sheets.

Noun

A *noun* is a word that names a thing such as an object, animal, place, person or feeling For example: shoe, dog, lake, child, sadness.

Prefix

A *prefix* is a group of letters placed before the root (base) word which alter the meaning of the word. They are not words in their own right and cannot stand on their own.

For example: redo, misunderstand, export, autobiography, precook, disobey, subtract, etc.

Suffix

A *suffix* is a set of letters that go at the end of a root (base) word, changing the meaning of the word.

For example: reliance, payment, beautiful, lovely, weakness, etc.

Syllables

A *syllable* is a beat of sound in a word.

For example, '*gracefully*' has three beats (**grace / ful / ly**) and '*perhaps*' has two beats (**per / haps**).

Verb

A *verb* is a doing word in a sentence to show physical or mental action and it can also show a state of being.

For example: Mary raced downstairs. The old lady was upset

Unstressed vowels

Unstressed vowels are vowel sounds (*a, e, i, o* or *u*) that are difficult to hear when a word is said out loud. An example of a word with unstressed vowel sounds is 'interest'. When we say interest, it sounds more like 'intrest'.

Appendix 2

Irregular Verbs Past Tense

Most verbs form the past tense by adding **'ed'**. Some verbs do not follow this regular pattern and these verbs are called *irregular* verbs.

Examples of some irregular verbs.

are / were
blow / blew
build / built
buy / bought
catch / caught
choose / chose
come / came
dig / dug
drink / drank
drive / drove
eat / ate
fall / fell
feed / fed
find / found
fly / flew
get /got
give / gave
go / went
hang / hung
have / had
hear / heard
hide / hid
hold / held
is /was
keep / kept

know / knew
leave / left
lends / lent
lose / lost
make / made
meet / met
put / put
read / read
ring / rang
run / ran
see / saw
sell / sold
send / sent
sing / sang
sit / sat
sleep / slept
speak / spoke
spend / spent
steal / stole
swim / swam
teach / taught
think / thought
wake / woke
win / won
write / wrote

Photo / Illustration Credits

Luggage label;
Graduation; Mohamed Hassan: Pixabay
Bus; Open Clipart Vectors: Pixabay
Dogs: Brilliant Publications Limited
Mountaineering
Fish; Ronny Overhate: Pixabay
Hippopotamus; Venita Oberholster: Pixabay
Doubts; Mohamed Hassan: Pixabay
Snake; Open Clipart Vectors: Pixabay
Cat: Brilliant Publications Limited
Secretary; Daniel Alvarado: Pixabay
Rat: Brilliant Publications Limited
Anzac Day; Tumisu: Pixabay
Vegetables; Open Clipart Vectors: Pixabay
Sailboat; Analogicus: Pixabay
Nurse; Clker-Free-Vector-Images: Pixabay
Elephant Sign; Bernis 74: Pixabay
Gardener; Mohamed Hassan: Pixabay
Classroom: Brilliant Publications Limited
Shop Window: Brilliant Publications Limited
WWII Women of Steel; Gary Butterfield: Unsplash
Nativity: Brilliant Publications Limited
Pair Cats: Brilliant Publications Limited
Pear: Brilliant Publications Limited
Stare: Brilliant Publications Limited
Stairs: Brilliant Publications Limited
Wail (image cropped and adjusted); Dmitry Abramov: Pixabay
Whale: Brilliant Publications Limited
Jigsaw; Clker-Free-Vector-Images: Pixabay
Dove; Dmitry Abramov: Pixabay

Page-top images:
Spelling Strategies – Hippopotamus; Dmitry Abramov: Pixabay
Keywords – Brilliant Publications Ltd
Suffixes – Weather Vane; Vizetelly: Pixabay
Functions of Suffixes – Pond; Clker Free Vector Images: Pixabay
Prefixes – Accident: Brilliant Publications Ltd
Root Words – Boy/dog tug-of-war; Agata: Pixabay
Spelling Rules – Sign post; Oberholster: Pixabay
Homophones – Sale or sail; Brilliant Publications Ltd
Silent Letters – Gnome; Oberholster Venita: Pixabay